There is a little corner of F
fertile rolling hills of Aquitain
of the
Massif Central and the glorious might of that fizzing city of the south, Toulouse. Nowadays it's been split into two rather uninspiring sounding *départements*. The Lot to the north and the Tarn et Garonne to the south. But this is an ancient land, ruled by its ancient capital, Cahors, and continuously inhabited for nearly three thousand years, as old as Rome. This rocky little scrap of French terrain is exceptionally beautiful and yet remains remarkably under populated. It was known then and is still known now as Le Quercy.

AMANDA LAWRENCE

White Stone Black Wine

LIFE AMONG THE ANCIENT VINEYARDS
OF THE QUERCY BLANC

Matador
9 De Montfort Mews
Leicester LE1 7FW, UK
Tel: (+44) 116 255 9311 / 9312
Email: books@troubador.co.uk
Web: www.troubador.co.uk/matador

ISBN 978-1906510-336

A Cataloguing-in-Publication (CIP) catalogue record for this book is available from the British Library.

Typeset in 11pt Bembo by Troubador Publishing Ltd, Leicester, UK
Printed in the UK by The Cromwell Press Ltd, Trowbridge, Wilts, UK

Matador is an imprint of Troubador Publishing Ltd

In memory of
The very dear man
Who took my tiny hand
And walked me round Cahors
In search of a highly elusive Papal Palace

Acknowledgements

Huge thanks to all those who pushed, encouraged and coerced me into finally finishing this book, they include Barbara Machin, Tessa Edwards, Kim Harvey and especially Christine Butler. Many thanks to Jeremy Thompson, Julia Fuller and Terry Compton for taking me on, sorting me out and never losing patience with me. Mille mercis to all my unfailingly hospitable friends and neighbours, who have dispensed reams of good advice, countless glasses of pastis and unwittingly starred in so many of the tales. Particular mention is due to the families Pelvillain, Treuille, Allet and Pugnière. Special thanks to my three beautiful daughters, Lucy, Felicity and Georgina, and to my ever-helpful son, Alexander. The lion's share of my gratitude, and innumerable bottles of the best Cahors, must of course be reserved for C – the beloved – without whom…

★★★

The people, places and events in this book are all real, but some of the names have been changed to protect the modest, whilst others have been deliberately kept to expose the gregarious.

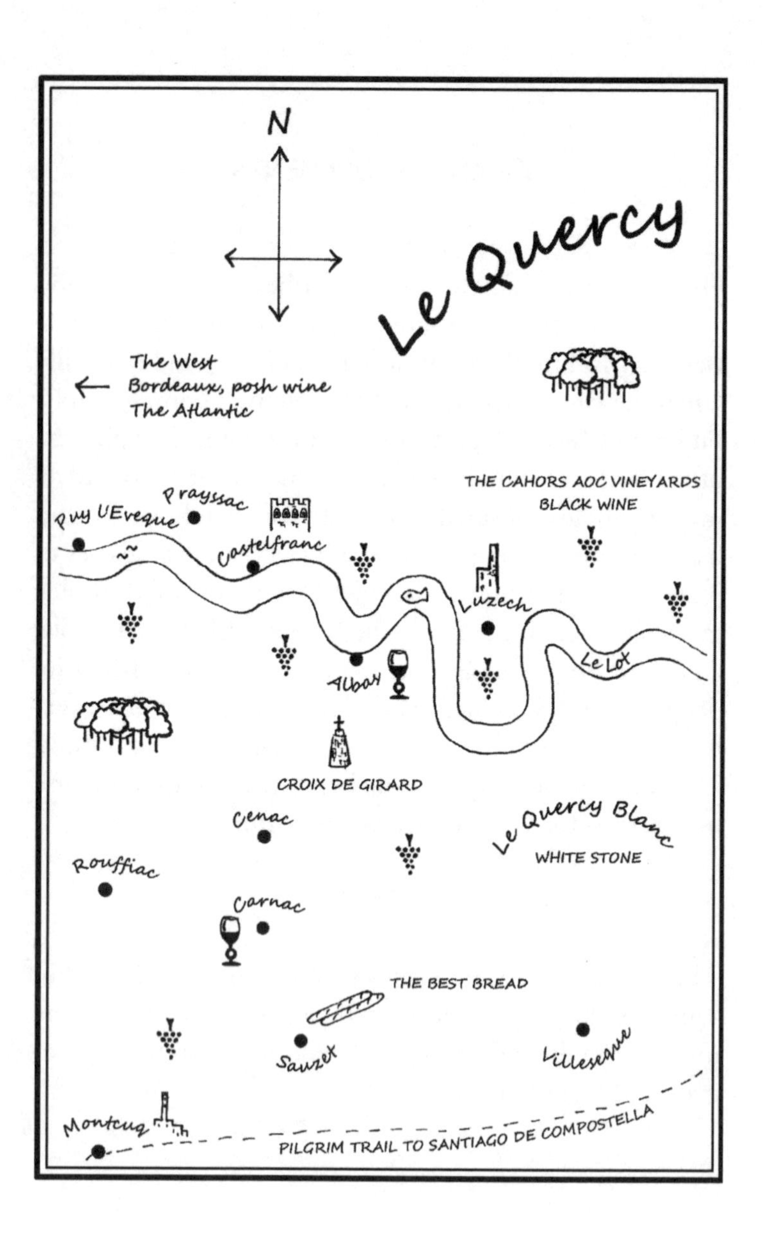
N
Le Quercy
The West
Bordeaux, posh wine
The Atlantic
THE CAHORS AOC VINEYARDS
BLACK WINE
Prayssac
Puy l'Eveque
Castelfranc
Luzech
Le Lot
Albas
CROIX DE GIRARD
Cenac
Le Quercy Blanc
WHITE STONE
Rouffiac
Carnac
THE BEST BREAD
Sauzet
Villeseque
Montcuq
PILGRIM TRAIL TO SANTIAGO DE COMPOSTELLA

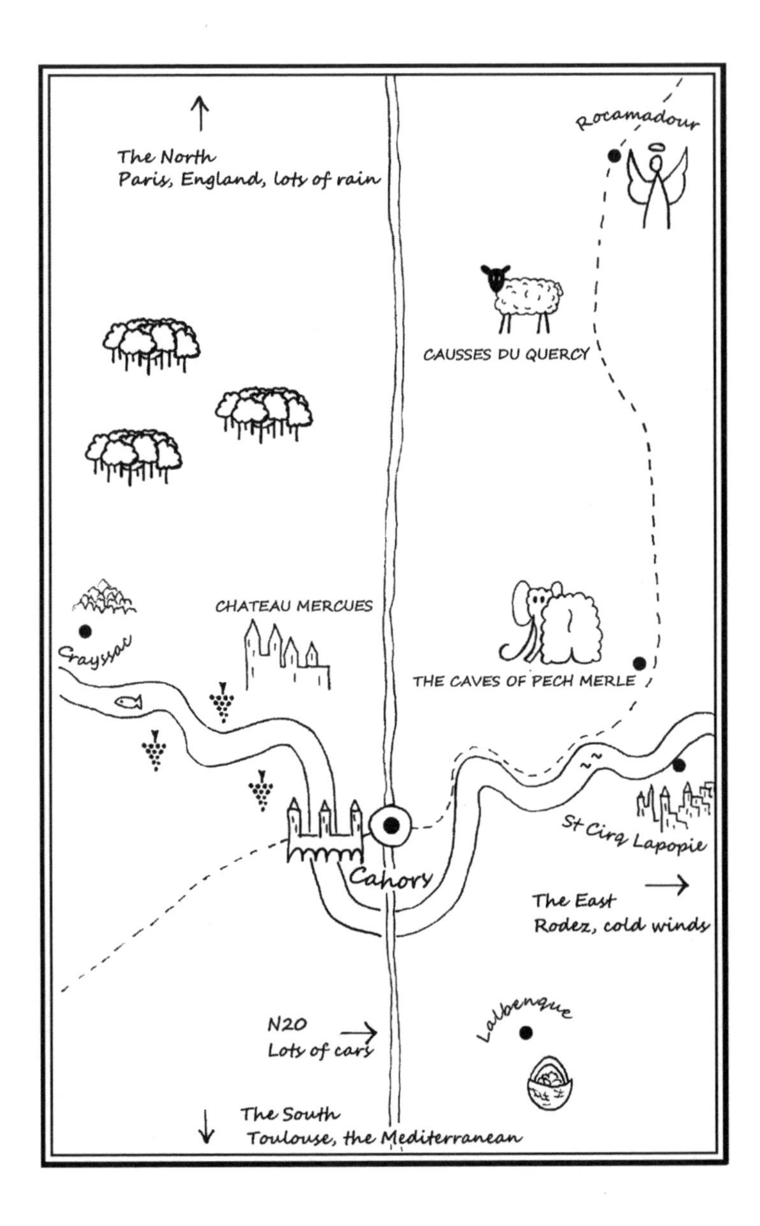
The North
Paris, England, lots of rain
Rocamadour
CAUSSES DU QUERCY
CHATEAU MERCUES
Crayssac
THE CAVES OF PECH MERLE
St Cirq Lapopie
Cahors
The East
Rodez, cold winds
Lalbenque
N20
Lots of cars
The South
Toulouse, the Mediterranean

Contents

Preface

"You'll need extra clouts today", my dear old grandmother used to murmur every other day, nodding sagely as if Socrates himself rarely uttered more sapient advice. Then she would button up her orange cardigan, with its one green button, and tuck her ears more firmly into the ridiculous knitted bonnet she used to wear whenever there was an r in the month, and frequently when there wasn't.

However on that cold, damp April morning as I forlornly surveyed a seemingly impenetrable blanket of forbidding grey cloud, heavy with rain, I could see exactly what she meant. Our half-acre of sodden Sussex countryside was shivery, dull and dolefully miserable. As far as the eye could see there was nothing but cloud, it was as if God, in puckish mood, had put a grimy, grey pudding basin over pudding-loving England.

I needed some sun and some warmth in my bones. I wanted to live in a place where clouts could be cast with gay abandon long before the may was even in bud. I yearned for the deep azure skies and brilliant light of southern Europe. I wanted to be able to stroll around a bustling market spilling with over-sized peppers and luscious peaches, to sit outside a street café in a village place in the early evening, sipping my Kir and perusing the menu. Most of all I wanted a place where I could live, work and put down roots that might have a chance of making contact with the soil, where seasonal treats are still truly seasonal.

It was time to move to a particular little corner of the south of France.

The south of France! Just saying the words gives me a sense

of warmth and well-being. Long years before we'd thought of buying our diminutive stone cottage we'd succumbed totally, completely and permanently to the captivating charms of ancient Quercy. But holidays were no longer enough, we didn't want to be tourists any more, the pull of the south and the siren song of the cicada had become too strong.

We wanted the Quercy to be home.

A
GAMBETTA
NE A CAHORS

The Evocative Sound Of Warm Southern Europe

The beloved drained the dregs of his *café noir,* shuffled the papers in his folder in meaningful style and informed me – as if I didn't know already - that we had a hot date with Guillaume.

We were lounging outside a sprawling café in beautiful, venerable Cahors, my favourite city in the world. A few metres away gallant Gambetta towered over the central place, cast in bronze. His brave army, once gathered around his feet, were gone now, desecrated by the Nazis. In their place a huge, curving fountain fell like a curtain announcing the star of the show, while curling around behind him a frothy backdrop of lavender wisteria bloomed riotously, rampaging over an immense pergola ten metres high and at least thirty metres long. The wars were long over, he didn't need his soldiers any more, these were much more peaceful guardians.

All around the *place* ancient stone buildings glowed softly in the late May sunshine, sublime on my chilly English shoulders. From the towering plane trees lining the boulevard I could hear the first of the season's cicadas announcing their presence, the percussion band of summer, and to me the wonderful, evocative sound of warm southern Europe.

I was in absolutely no rush; I could have lingered there all afternoon. After all this was France, no starchy waiter would hurry me on, no hovering client would demand my seat, nobody would mind at all.

The beloved slid a five-euro note under the ashtray and danced his eyebrows at me. Well, one person perhaps.

We'd met Guillaume before; he's an *immobilier*, although he really doesn't look like one. In England estate agents are a sober-suited bunch who think they're outrageously dressed if they wear a pink tie. Guillaume doesn't wear pink ties of course. He doesn't wear ties at all; as a matter of fact I've only once seen him wear a shirt. Most of the time he's resplendent in jeans and a black T-shirt, to match his carefully tousled ink-black hair.

We had an appointment to view a house somewhere in the hills between Cahors and Puy l'Evêque – a distance of about thirty kilometres. No estate agent in France will give you the exact location of any house you're interested in. If you're lucky they may possibly mention the nearest village or town – once they've got you in their office of course – but that's as far as they'll go in pinpointing the spot, if you want any more information you'll have to arrange an escorted visit. The reason for this extreme caution is really very simple, estate agents charge an absolute fortune for their services and no vendor in his right mind would think of giving his business to just one. Why put all your eggs in one basket when for exactly the same amount you can have every basket in town? So every property has at least three or four agents, often more. If the immobilier wants to secure his commission he simply must ensure that he, or his lieutenant, not only introduces, but also escorts and negotiates with the eventual buyer. That way there's absolutely no doubt about the division of spoils. It's an unsatisfactory system but until the French catch on to the idea of the sole-agent deal, or the Internet revolution forces a review of the pricing policy, I'm very much afraid it will stay that way.

It turned out that our prospective house-in-the-hills was not very far – Guillaume informed us even more cautiously – from Sauzet. We could hardly believe our ears, Sauzet is the nearest village to our little stone two-up, one-and-a-bit-down holiday cottage, and whilst living in one, we planned to rent out the other to like-minded Francophiles in search of a slice of rural paradise. This would be a perfect location. The property immediately whizzed up our list of favourites. The man of the moment caught the gleam in my eye and sprang out of his tubular chair, a vision in casual chic. We would follow him. There was just one thing he thought we should know, (uh-oh) he took a deep breath and informed us that the house 'wasn't quite clean'. We nodded absently, wondering just how dirty it could possibly be if it was still being lived in. He exchanged a brief, high-speed conversation with his slender-hipped assistant, in which I only caught the words kitchen, laundry and woodpile, then gravely warned us again that the house really wasn't in great condition and not at all clean. He wasn't exaggerating.

We set off in tandem from his offices in Puy L'Evêque and proceeded at breakneck speed through the raked vineyards and sunflower fields of the Lot valley, shooting past almost sheer cliffs that threatened to tumble over at any moment – or so the ominous road signs seem to indicate – and eventually up into the oak-forested hills beyond. The roads narrowed pretty alarmingly at this point, though Guillaume's speed hardly reflected the fact, and as we gradually climbed out of the last straggling morning mists in the river valley, we burst into blazing sunshine and had to shade our eyes whilst desperately trying to keep his skidding rear wheels in view.

Seemingly deserted stone hamlets flashed past. Venerable churches stood proud on craggy outcrops, with a few cottages huddled close to the walls and the ubiquitous memorial to the lost sons of the community, sober reminders of a violent past, not so very long ago. We sped round chalky hairpins, not quite in a cloud of dust but it felt that way, then past vineyards the size of a bed sheet and walnut groves clinging tenaciously to the rocky slopes. Every now and then an old *paysan* could be seen, back bent like a hook, attending to the last of the spring chores, but it was too early in the year for any real activity in the vineyards and the land was deserted, waiting for the coming of summer.

At last Guillaume's Golf came to an abrupt halt, just round one of the hairpins and right on the edge of an impressive drop. He disentangled himself from the steering wheel and bounced towards us. For a few seconds I allowed my heart to stop thumping and wondered idly if he'd run out of petrol, since there was clearly no dwelling anywhere near. He leaned in my passenger window and pointed halfway up the hill on the far side of the valley.

"That is it," he announced, shortly.

I squinted through the dusty windscreen, and then got out for a better view.

"What, that little château-type place? Are you sure?" I stared at the imposing façade in the distance and made all sorts of hasty, thoroughly ill-advised decisions in my mind before I'd got within barking distance of it.

He grinned. He's good at his job.

We drove on for at least another three kilometres before we came to the house itself. From the entrance – at the back, which is the usual point of access in the Quercy – the view was not quite as impressive. In fact it looked more like the sort of place Joseph would have rejected in favour of the stable. It is an unusual house to English eyes as it's constructed on the side of a very steep hill, so from one side it looks as if all the accommodation – such as it is – is on one level, whilst from the other it looks absolutely vast. The truth of course, is somewhere in between.

We climbed out and stretched our legs whilst Guillaume fumbled with multiple keys. The setting was glorious, a vast panoramic view with vine-covered hills rising behind, and oak woods spreading on two sides. Unfortunately the house was not quite so fetching. Inside it had been decorated in vivid bougainvillea pinks and purples mixed with rag-rolled yellow – the exact colour of The Simpsons' skin. Most of the bedrooms sported faded orange walls and curtains of a shimmering mauve.

"Interesting decoration!" Guillaume ventured euphemistically and gave me a rueful grin.

Downstairs the situation was even worse, there was junk everywhere, but that wasn't the main issue, the building didn't seem to be altogether finished. There were bare stone walls and chipped plasterboard all over the place. Obviously the owner had divided this basement portion into the required number of rooms and got no further. On the lower terrace there was even an abandoned old Citroën. The beloved gave me a speaking glance that said, "No way!"

Back upstairs our indomitable agent was opening the floor length shutters in the drawing room and exposing the full glory of the view. The house hung over a dizzy vista of the Lot valley, taking in artfully spread vineyards, oak forests, river valleys and ancient stone hamlets. I drew a deep breath; Cézanne himself could hardly have bettered it.

The drawing room was a good size too, with magnificent broad chestnut beams and a vast *cheminée*. As Guillaume threw open the final shutters the beloved's initial hasty opinions began to undergo a subtle change. Two pairs of French windows opened onto a southwest facing upper terrace about fifteen metres long. The almost wild garden fanned out before us. I peered cautiously over at collapsed, ancient stone terraces holding back precarious scrub oaks and innumerable rosemary, helichrysum and juniper bushes. Huge lavenders billowed and blew in the warm breeze. I leaned over a bit further. Far below us, the valley rang with laughter as three burly vignerons enjoyed a good joke, a good litre of the usual and a few

Gauloises before going home for a leisurely two-hour lunch.

"Look, you see that tower?" Our hero cried, bouncing perilously off the wooden balusters and pointing into the milky blue distance. "That's Tournon D'Agenais!"

Tournon is thirty kilometres away and, as a matter of fact I couldn't make out exactly which bit of landscape he meant, but he'd made his point and he knew it. The plasterboard and paint could be changed; the views and location couldn't.

Guillaume smiled as he watched me frantically scribbling on the back of the photocopied details. People don't bother to make copious notes if they're not interested.

"Perhaps you come and work for me when you live 'ere, eh?" He enquired speculatively. Yes perhaps, after a two-year crash-diet, a six-month crash-course in colloquial French, a hundred sessions with Toni and Guy and *carte blanche* at the nearest Gap boutique.

What is it about the French and style? They seem to exude it so effortlessly. My thoughts drifted back to our young neighbour in Rouffiac. Juliette was only six and as dirty, boisterous and hair-in-a-tangle untidy as any six year-old. But there was a charm about her, an air. Her clothes were rarely expensive but always chic. Her eyes were either alive with enthusiasm or shyly lowered with an engaging bashfulness. When confronted with a formal greeting her manners were impeccable. Never did she exhibit any lack of style. She was born that way.

Having waved our *immobilier* goodbye and resisted his generous invitation to go back to his office with him and be talked into signing something extremely unwise, we decided to meander down to the river and take a look at the nearest village. We knew Sauzet, about four kilometres to the south, it's home to a cosy local *auberge* and also has a splendid *boulangerie*. But three kilometres north – as the crow flies – on the river itself, the nearest village to this property is Albas and strangely, we'd never seen it.

It was Albas that tipped the wavering scales for me, with limitless charm on its side. In a region full of turreted old stone villages, this is one of the prettiest of all. It was just after noon when we first arrived and the locals were at lunch. The pale grey village dozed in the sun and the old school on the far side of the *place* had half closed its shutters against the penetrating light. On one side of the village the cliffs rise sharply, venerable cottages desperately clinging to the edge. On the other, the indigo river, far below, mirrors the ancient stones. Apart from the school there is an old church, a part-time post office and of course the mairie, which precariously tops a pinnacle of rock and looks about to slide into the river below at any moment. There's a medieval tangle of houses, a pretty little restaurant festooned with geraniums, a bar and a *boulangerie*. That's it. It's not at all affluent. The ancient houses have chipped and crumbling stonework adorned with peeling shutters. The *boulangerie* doesn't advertise itself in the correct place, but then if you live there you know where it is, and if you don't it doesn't matter anyway. The whole place is very small, crammed into a tiny niche in the looming cliffs. It will never grow any bigger, there's no room.

This was the village where our two younger children would go to school; it would be our local *boulangerie* and the site for the local fêtes. We tried to keep an open mind, after all this was only the first of eleven potential *maisons charmante*, but secretly I already knew, there was a familiar feeling in my bones and, despite my best efforts, plans were beginning to form.

A month or so later, back in the land of toast and Marmite, we received a phone call from our esteemed agent. To say that he was panicking would be to wildly understate the situation. Our vendors had another buyer.

"Well we always knew that was the case", the beloved had tried to reason with him. "They're not likely to sell though are they? They told us they'd had another offer and it was just too low – that was weeks ago – we've offered considerably more haven't we?"

"Listen!" Guillaume responded, "This man has been putting on the very heavy pressure all day, *c'est une catastrophe!*" He underlined every English word and lapsed into French in between, he was almost incomprehensible with panic. This was entirely our fault; we should have signed that unwise document in the first place, now he was in danger of losing his commission! We must immediately do something to ward off the horrendous consequences of our scandalously casual behaviour.

The beloved tried to placate him. Surely if they were going to sell to another buyer they would already have done so by this time? They were probably just trying to pressurise us into getting a move-on.

It transpired that our rival was a local man who had taken to dropping in on our vendors to try to persuade them to sell to him. He was apparently offering to go with them to the *notaire's* office the next morning to sign the *compromis de vente*. We had to ring the vendors ourselves *immédiatement*, it was *impérative*, we had to reassure them that we were serious buyers and then we must, simply must, sign the *achat de vente* that Guillaume had so kindly sent us, if not, well the consequences were just too dire to contemplate, all would be lost!

We put the phone down on the excitable Guillaume and tried to discuss the situation calmly. It certainly sounded serious; if there really was another buyer and he was local we were at a distinct disadvantage. However, we reasoned, Guillaume would move heaven and earth to keep this wayward ball in the air, and in the meantime we would consult our wickedly expensive legal eagle – whom we'd nicknamed Dawn French – partly because she happened to have the same Christian name as the witty comedienne and partly for obvious reasons. It was almost midnight, nothing more could be done until the morning. We retired to bed and tossed and turned till – well – dawn.

The desperately expensive Dawn saved the day. Dear she may have been, dilatory she certainly was not. I've never met anybody more on the ball in my life. She'd grasped the essentials of the situation, turned them around, explained the surprisingly simple solution and issued instructions by phone, e-mail and fax before we had time to catch our breath.

The beloved phoned Guillaume with the good news. It seemed we suddenly had a home in France.

The next few months were taken up with completing the reams of paperwork deemed necessary for such a leap of faith, and filing the remainder in the bin. Which rather proved we'd chosen the right country for our enterprise. Our two younger children had to sever their links with friends at school, and prepare to learn a new language, go to a new school and make new friends. An uphill task when you're only ten or eleven. The two elder children, grown up and about to fly the nest anyway, decided this might be a good time to tentatively spread their wings.

So it was that we eventually found ourselves with one daughter in England, one in Spain and the ten-year-old in France with us, along with our eleven-year-old son. All of a sudden we had become a cosmopolitan family. This would take a bit of getting used to.

One mild summer day, we finally loaded the remains of our English life into our faithful old Volkswagen Passat, perched the children on top of piles of bedding and, squeezing the reluctant doors shut, set off for Dover and a new beginning.

We parked obediently in an expectant, over-heated grid of about five hundred cars. Nearly all had their engines impatiently running, exuding enough poisonous fumes to create a hole the size of Scotland in the fragile ozone layer, just in case they were suddenly waved forward to the ferry.

Despite this obvious blight, Dover has atmosphere. The port may be a little larger and a little more sophisticated but it really hasn't changed very much since Michael Caine waved three Mini Coopers on board ship, ostensibly bound for a gold heist in Italy. There is still that balled up feeling of suppressed excitement about it. Of course it's the gateway to that mysterious landmass known for centuries to the inhabitants of our island kingdom as 'The Continent'. Slightly exotic, culturally different, linguistically varied, gastronomically superior and above all, warm! Which was exactly why our four hundred and ninety-nine gas-guzzling neighbours were going there. They rustled maps, opened flasks and bundled children in and out of back seats, chattering excitedly all the while.

We sat back reflectively; it wasn't quite the same for us. We had our reasons for going to this foreign land too, they didn't quite match those of our holidaymaking compatriots, but we weren't worlds apart.

In fact the main difference was a small one. We didn't have a return ticket.

* * *

The Art Of Bureaucracy

The bleached stone walls of the old convent were warm and inviting and a solitary lime-green lizard basked luxuriously on the rough-hewn basement sill in the early summer sun. It was a radiant morning in the last days of June and the sun was pleasantly hot on my bare shoulders as I scrabbled in the rocks to make a large enough hole for the new vine I hoped to train along the southern wall.

By this time we were ensconced in our tiny, tumbledown stone cottage, waiting for the purchase of the larger house to go through. I'd been up and about very early, weeding the herb garden, pottering round the lavenders and watching my lizard emerge from his crevice in the old stones to a flat white surface where he could spread his toes and unashamedly expose himself. The hamlet was deserted; the few adults were at work, the even fewer children – including ours – that lived in this tiny, half-forgotten place, were at school. The enormous silence was so complete I could hear every squeak and creak. And it was whilst I was bent, bum skywards, amongst the thigh-high basil that I heard an utterly unfamiliar 'tick, tick'. Peering round the tallest bit of verbiage I was somewhat startled to find a pair of hoopoes walking calmly up the narrow lane, less than six feet away from me, pecking at ants or other minor snacks as they went. I scarcely dared breathe. My posture wasn't exactly a comfortable one either, certainly not to be recommended for bird watching. I sank as quietly as possible to my creaking knees, and turned again. They paid me no more attention than if I'd been a moss covered chunk of old rock – which I suppose I could well have resembled, with my filthy knees and olive green T-shirt – just strutted proudly past, their magnificent long crests curving smoothly downwards to match their long beaks, making them look – as the beloved observed later that day – as if their heads would work both ways. They walked the entire length of the tiny *place* and disappeared behind the little chapel.

I scuttled back to the kitchen, thrilled, and recounted the mini-adventure to the afore-mentioned. He was equally impressed and we crept out to skirt the chapel in order to catch another glimpse of them. This was a little too much for their fragile equilibrium and after a few nervous glances they took off for more peaceful and congenial surroundings on the other side of our neighbour's crumbling barn. We returned to the cottage delighted with ourselves, and more than ready for a large bowl of *café crème* and a crumb of breakfast, only to find, *quel horreur*! The gas had run out.

Leaving the hoopoes to their ants we decided to enjoy a quick sojourn at a local café for our *petit déjeuner* – one of the truly great pleasures of French life – swapping the gas bottle at the same time.

You would think this would be a pretty straightforward

procedure. After all, most of rural France runs on bottled gas and every little village shop and garage is stocked with numerous coloured bottles. However we hadn't taken into consideration the French passion for copious documentation. Our bottle was eventually accepted, and we were issued with two cubes; squat, square shaped bottles that fit more easily into modern kitchens. And, of course, because there are two of them you can be sure you never run out during a public holiday.

"*Bon idée*, we'll take them", we told the girl.

"*Non*", she informed us firmly; first we must fill in a form.

We did so, now could we have our cubes?

"*Non*", now it must be authorised and then signed.

"Just for a bottle of gas?" I asked, somewhat ill advisedly, and was treated to a look that could have withered forests.

But our gradual initiation into the French love of bureaucracy told us we were unlikely to get anything at all if we didn't comply. We meekly did as we were told. Now could we have our cubes? "*Mais bien sûr*", nothing would afford her greater pleasure. If we would just sign this copy of the form, and this one, and then this one and finally this one.

We took our bottles and withdrew to the café for a restorative coffee and a crisp, buttery croissant.

*

Two days later the beloved announced his avowed intent to install a telephone in Le Pigeonnier, as the cottage is known.

The Quercy is famous for its *pigeonniers*; every farmhouse has one and every village has at least one, usually two or three and sometimes more. They're turreted stone-built towers, often built onto the side of the house to accommodate the pigeons that used to be bred for meat, and in many country properties still are. Quercy architecture generally reserves the cool ground floor of the house for the animals, food, wine and various other stores, whilst only the first floor is equipped for human habitation. This is reached by an outside stone stairway known as a *bolet*. Therefore a *pigeonnier* often had completely separate access and its earthen floor was frequently used for the famous ducks and geese of the region. Our little stone holiday cottage had once been the village *four á pain*, the communal bread oven. Now it had been converted and enlarged and, like many others, modified to make the *pigeonnier* an integral part of the house.

One thing it definitely lacked, though, was a telephone. Our ever-helpful neighbour, Hélène, offered to ring France Telecom for us to arrange the whole. This was lazily tempting but we decided that if we were going to live and work in this little corner of the world, the sooner we learned to stand on our own four feet, the better.

The Telecom office is in the centre of Cahors, and we rolled in ten minutes before noon to try our luck.

"Ah, er… *Bonjour M'sieur*", my hero began, putting on his best French accent, "*parlez-vous Anglais peut-être*?"

"*Non*" stated the bored-looking official. He leaned one elbow on the counter, stuck his chin out and looked us insolently up and down. It wasn't a promising start.

"Ah!" The beloved glanced at me, I could see the iron resolve in the man beginning to assert itself. We explained in our somewhat meagre French, more or less what we wanted and the bored-looking official immediately came to life and started to fire questions at the usual missile speed. We concentrated hard. Passports? Well actually we'd left them at home, '*très désolé*'.

What about a *Carte de séjour*? Well actually no, they're no longer necessary you see... We were, we belatedly realised, inadequately prepared.

We were frog marched to a computer screen and told to

repeat our names and address. Unfortunately we couldn't remember our postcode. The official sighed loudly and looked it up for us.

"*D'accord*", our telephone would be fitted in two weeks time, which day would be convenient? Ah. Actually we had to return to England that week. He looked at us as if his life had been immeasurably shortened by the crass stupidity of these *Anglais*.

"We have a neighbour..." I ventured apologetically.

He sighed, and started to fill in Hélène's details.

"Her telephone number?"

I squirmed. That was in the phone book, which unfortunately we seemed to have left behind. He grabbed the *Pages Blanches* and thumbed through them moodily. I was heartily relieved to see Hélène and Francois' number there. God only knows what would have happened if they'd been ex-directory.

The relevant information was tapped in. He handed us a scrap of paper with our new number on it and informed us that the men would be in our hamlet on the 16th. He then dismissed us with a curt nod.

"*C'est tout*."

We positively scurried across the boulevard and collapsed into chairs outside the café, tingling with embarrassment. It was five past twelve. Of course! All became immediately clear. Any problem can be overcome in France if it avoids a lunchtime delay. We sat back in the warm sun and began to relax; after all, we'd done it. At times the whole episode had reached the stage of a classic farce, but we'd done it – and in French. The embarrassing tingle was replaced by a warm glow. We had absolutely no right to; but we really felt rather proud.

★

The phone was duly installed and life settled down into a gentle, outdoor routine, enlivened by numerous long meals and the antics of our two bachelor neighbours.

"I think", the beloved intoned gravely over the morning coffee cups, "that we ought to have a dinner party."

I very nearly dropped my brioche in my lap. This was not like him, not like him at all. Before asking the inevitable, I thought it politic to agree fervently and possibly get the request down in black and white.

"Wonderful idea," I finally managed to squeak, "it's ages since we had one… who were you thinking of inviting, is there a reason?" For this highly uncharacteristic behaviour, I could have added. Have you gone mad; is it the sun?

He stretched back in his chair and explained: We'd been living in our stone holiday cottage for several weeks, gradually putting our new life into some sort of order and waiting until the beginning of October when we would officially own our château-cum-tumbledown stable. During this time we'd relied pretty heavily on the help, unstinting advice and easily given friendship of our near neighbours. We ought to repay them and a dinner party indoors in our tiny cottage was quite unthinkable, so we needed to plan for a big party out in the square in guaranteed sunshine; in other words August. We had ten days left.

Invitations were issued and accepted for the following Saturday and the barbecue was to be given a thorough makeover for the occasion.

Posh barbecues are not a feature of the little villages in this part of France. Ours is a dilapidated affair with collapsible legs and a base like tin foil. But our neighbour, Gilles beats that hands down. When he has a party, the long wooden trestle tables are laid out in the late afternoon and nothing else happens until at least nine o'clock. Then all of a sudden the square springs into life. Half a dozen dusty old cars, in varying stages of decay, race into the hamlet and shoehorn themselves into the shadiest spots. Gilles produces an old oil drum; his wife, Françoise unrolls twenty feet of paper cloth on the tables and sets a jug of sunflowers, a pitcher of water and a bottle of pastis in the centre. A whoosh and a cry and three-foot high flames issue from the drum. Gilles flaps around a bit, the flames die down, Françoise brings out the delicious *entrées* and the party commences. A good, relaxed hour or so later, four whole chickens emerge on an old iron poker – doing temporary service as a spit – and Gilles sits entirely at his ease at one end of the table, laughing, talking and efficiently emptying glass after glass of potent Cahors wine with one hand, whilst lazily turning the spit with the other.

That's the way to conduct a barbecue! We weren't quite in his class yet.

Saturday morning saw me at the fresh fish counter in one of the large supermarkets. I wanted some tuna and they happened to have a whole fish on display, five feet long and staring me balefully in the eye. This isn't particularly unusual and I'm a bit of a sucker for a magnificent beast like this. All the same, they probably only appear whole every couple of weeks or so and only at certain times of the year – when the tuna shoals arrive on the Basque coast. I felt I'd been particularly lucky but I was very soon to be disillusioned.

I asked the fishmonger for five *belle tranches*. There would be ten for dinner, but a good slice of tuna is certainly too much for one person, especially if you're expecting him to eat another two or three courses afterwards.

From behind the splendid creature the *homme* in charge – for the sake of *entente cordiale* we'll call him a fishmonger – produced five skinny grey slices and held them out for my approval. I sighed and summoned both courage and the best of my French.

Unfortunately the irritating *poissonier* knew quite well that he had me on the run. The cut slices must be sold first, it was in the rules and he didn't make the rules, he was just doing his job. I told him I didn't want them. But I had asked for them, *et voila*! There they were, five slices, indisputably. I squirmed. I hate this kind of confrontation, but I had to stick to my guns, I didn't want them. I wanted five freshly cut, thick slices from the new fish. We argued. He brought in reinforcements from the management and I collapsed in a steaming, simmering heap under the pressure of a torrent of bureaucratic health, safety and sacred profit margin French. All the same I wasn't going to accept his skinny grey offerings. I gathered myself together with as much dignity as I could muster and nodded goodbye to the highly entertained queue behind me. To the market!

Mid-August must surely be one of the most agreeable times of the year to visit a French market. Of course I'm not the only one who thinks so, the market place was thronged with tourists. I threaded my way through vast cameras and up-to-the-minute pastel-coloured outfits, through the early stalls of peaches and melons, past the flower sellers with their armfuls of colourful statice, purple, white, pink and gold, then on to the centre and serious business part of the market. Here you'll find the best of the vegetable stalls, the *boucherie* vans and the *fromageries* and of course the wonderful thirty-foot fish stall. At one end the toothless, elderly dame who looks after the crustacean side of things was shovelling kilos of glistening mussels. Beside them piles of rubber-banded lobsters were enthusiastically demonstrating their freshness, and a Mont Blanc of fresh ice was being heaped round them to cool their ardour. But at the back, amongst the larger and more expensive fish, I spied the current object of my desire. It was getting late by this time and there wasn't much left, perhaps a quarter of the fish, possibly less. I examined the new candidate while I waited my turn. This *poissonerie* is always incredibly busy. It isn't cheap, but it's very good. The Cadurciennes like their fish fresh, they also like to have it boned or skinned on demand, they like to be able to direct the action and they're prepared to pay extra for the privilege. Naturally this just makes it even busier, because while the old lady in the blue print pinny has her small *rouget* carefully filleted, the queue buckles behind her. I asked for my five slices and added that I would appreciate it if I could have five fresh ones, not the first slice, it looked a bit dry and after all this was August. There was no question. Would I like my slices one centimetre thick, or two, or a little more? My fish was cut to my exact specifications. It was firm, dark red and succulent. A lemon was added to the bag and a long sprig of fennel completed the bounty. I handed over all the money I had about my person at that time and almost danced back through the crowds.

After a quick visit to the hole-in-the-wall, sited conveniently and unobtrusively in an ancient stone arch on the edge of the market square, I consulted my list. Fragrant aromas lured me to the fruit stall where one of my neighbours was in temporary charge of affairs – his friend was away, he explained, he had stepped into the breach – what would I like? I bought huge, juicy peaches, streaked like the dawn. I bought a kilo of the amazingly sweet strawberries, Mara des Bois, and to start the meal in a light and stress-free fashion, two Quercynois melons. Now for some *charcuterie* to go with them. I usually buy my meat from the little stalls, local farmers, but when you want a good Bayonne ham it's best to go to one of the big *charcuterie* lorries that tour these markets. They're still pretty local but they're specialists and you know you'll find exactly what you're looking for. I watched the wafer-thin pink shreds curl down onto the paper. Twenty slices, as thin as tracing paper, and with that distinctive nutty flavour that defines a good Bayonne. A feast.

Some unctuous cheese was next on the list. A little care is

needed when buying cheese in a market, you're quite likely to be waylaid by stallholders holding out sample slivers of delicious cheeses from the high Causses or somewhere equally impressive, and they're often charging way over the odds for it. You can find yourself nodding in approval, find he's cut you a substantial slice, and before you know what's hit you you're handing over twenty or thirty euros for something you had no intention of buying in the first place. I gave them a wide berth and headed towards the *fromagerie* from Rocamadour. This famous goat's cheese is one of the delicacies of the area and adorns every cheese platter from Souillac to Montauban. It's also spectacularly good grilled and dressed with olive oil in a warm goat's cheese salad. I needed it for the former and bought five pungent, creamy discs. A different *fromagerie* for the Bleu des Causses, another local speciality, some ripe, runny Brie and a large crumbly slice of Laguiole – a salty farmhouse version of Cantal, similar to good Cheddar – completed the selection. All that remained was the salad. I made my way to a tiny stall that sits rather worryingly close to the Leonidas chocolate shop. Lettuces were running short as it was well after midday by this time. I asked if she had any Batavia *rouge*. Yes, she did, in a box in the shade. Did I want a green one as well? They were 45 cents each.

"Or three for a euro," she smiled. I bought three. She brought out another box of huge, misshapen tomatoes and yet another of *mâche* – lambs lettuce – then filled the spaces in my basket with scarlet radishes and a bunch of lemony sorrel. I still had change from my five-euro note.

My favourite *boulangerie* is on the Boulevard de Gambetta, right in the centre of town, I stopped for four of their particularly slender, golden baguettes, *pain aux noix* – walnut bread – and a small but delectable *tarte aux poireaux*, for lunch. A highly successful conclusion to the blush-making events in the supermarket.

That evening saw us gathered in a convivial group around Gilles' trestle table – borrowed for the occasion - in the slanting shade of the little chapel at the centre of the square. I had borrowed Françoise's sunflower jug too, and placed a litre bottle of Ricard at the other end of the table. It was one of their new sunny summer bottles, opaque yellow glass with the distinctive blue logo, it simply breathes the south of France.

The melon and Bayonne ham had more than lived up to their respective reputations and conversation had subsided as our guests concentrated on the subtle flavours. The last drop of walnut oil was soaked up by the last of the *pain aux noix*, the dark red wines were poured, glasses clinked and everybody relaxed, the edges off their appetites. Lengthening shadows indicated that the sun was low on the horizon, turning the sky Prussian blue, lavender and gold. I sat at the end of the table and watched the beloved performing his party piece with the tuna. In the cool, dark interior of our cottage, the laden cheese board waited to make its entrance. The Brie – as Bries will, in high summer – had been behaving like a recalcitrant child and had already run away twice. Beside it the strawberries topped little *barquettes* of sweet pastry, mascarpone and crème fraîche. The peaches, in their glazed terracotta bowl, rested outside on the stone wall, soaking up the late sun.

"First sitting!" The beloved cried, waving his fish slice about like a scimitar. "Who likes it rare?"

At the far end of the table the teenage contingent were in a world of their own, gazing into liquid eyes, stroking each other's suntans and picking the garlic off their tuna.

"*Les patates ma chère*?" François nudged me and handed over the bowl of baby potatoes and chopped black olives, drenched in olive oil and lemon juice. I bit into the juicy tuna the beloved had just placed on my plate, pink in the middle, crisply barbecued outside. A peppery tang from the sorrel salad, a few sips of glowing, dark wine and I leaned back in deep satisfaction. Delicious.

★

One of the banes of modern-day living is the ever present need for valid insurance. Car insurance, house insurance, health insurance, just-about-anything-worth-having insurance; I find it incredibly irritating. The French, in true Gallic style, have added a neat little codicil to this burden. If you want to change your car insurance from one company to another you may only do so if you have given the current insurers at least two months notice.

"Two months!" The beloved echoed in horrified French with a very English accent.

"*Oui Monsieur, c'est normal.*" The slender little man behind the desk gave him a sheaf of papers and asked for his passport.

This is a common occurrence in France. For a start, unless using the ubiquitous credit card one has to prove one's identity all the time, from the supermarket check-out to the *immobiliers* office, to the local branch of France Telecom. A passport is the handiest document for doing so. The point, I suppose, is that the British, like the Americans have become a nation of consumers. We buy, reinvent, throw away and buy new, constantly. The French haven't quite got there yet, especially in the country. A new car means little as a status symbol in France; it merely means the old one's finally given up the struggle. A large house generally reflects a large extended family, not a large income. As for a yacht or some equally expensive macho item, that means you're probably a bit mad. With the obvious exceptions of good, hardwearing clothes, good haircuts and good food, the rural French don't buy unless they have to.

The little man cleared his throat and looked enquiringly at us.

"Oh all right then," the beloved grumped, "I suppose we'd better stick with you."

"*Bien Monsieur,*" he replied, smiling for the first time that afternoon, and set to work stamping, signing, copying and otherwise generating the huge pile of unnecessary paperwork that keeps a Frenchman just this side of the consumer tracks.

The beloved glanced forlornly at the clock; it was almost six.

"D'you suppose the café will still be serving drinks?" He asked me, which seemed a superfluous question, as they never stop doing just that.

"I'm sure they will," I answered soothingly, scrabbling about in my bag for my passport. Oh dear, he had badly wanted to change the car insurance. After days of Internet research and hours of chatting to the neighbours about just who was best – and cheapest – it turned out it was all for nothing. We had, as usual, left it too late and French bureaucracy had had the last laugh.

Pass The Orange Box

Half a dozen grizzled gentlemen in well-washed *bleu* and battered berets were lazily playing *pétanque*, or sitting at their ease on iron benches, happily pickling their tonsils with pastis. They had the best spot in the village of course, under the shade of the pollarded plane trees. One or two looked up and nodded or raised a horny finger in salute as we trundled through the little medieval village of Sauzet, parched and dusty white in the early evening sun. We were on our way to what was to become a wild night out in every sense of the word.

Having been resident in the Quercy for a bare twelve weeks we were thrilled when we received an invitation to a local barbeque, a *déjeuner sur l'herbe*, to meet our prospective new neighbours. It was explained that the highly eccentric *fermier* who owned the ancient stone *maison de maître* further up the hill was holding his annual *fin de saison* party. Our imminent arrival amongst their tiny community had been announced and we were required to present ourselves for inspection, approval and formal introductions.

The instructions were to meet at the house of another neighbour beforehand, ostensibly for a quick aperitif, but principally in case we got horribly lost.

"Any time after seven-thirty", we were told.

We arrived in good time, our first blunder.You quickly learn – not quite quickly enough in our case – that in rural France an invitation to drinks at seven-thirty means sometime after eight. An invitation to dinner at eight means arrive some time after eight-thirty, preferably nine. Greetings will take twenty minutes or so, essential talk will take at least another twenty minutes, then aperitifs will appear. Some time after nine-thirty the pastis and ratafia, whisky and Muscat will be abandoned for the pleasures of the table, but if you weren't prepared you may well be horizontal by this time.

We eventually set off, just as the sun was setting over silhouetted peaks, and trekked steadily upwards through dense scrub and knee-high blond grasses. It was harder work than my lamentable knees had been used to for the last twenty years and conversation lapsed as we puffed in single file towards the house on the crest of the hill. By the time we were halfway, my thigh and calf muscles were whimpering in panic and the aforementioned decrepit knees eventually gave up the fight and went on strike. I trailed forlornly an embarrassing forty feet behind the others.

The cicadas – blissfully unaware of my plight – serenaded us from the treetops whilst crickets, small frogs and heaven knows what else leapt hurriedly out of our way. It gradually began to dawn on us that we were walking not merely because it was close enough to do so, but because there was no road to the house and therefore no choice in the matter.

We finally arrived heaving and gasping at the scene of the action just as twilight was beginning to fade. A group of about forty rural Frenchmen swivelled to inspect us, Gauloises wagging, pastis suspended between hand and mouth in silent astonishment. I felt like a tart in a W.I. meeting, and not the jam variety either.

The beloved ploughed in with his very best French. He's much braver than I am in these confrontational situations, and although his French is a trifle basic, he speaks with such an obviously English accent it really doesn't matter. Allowances are made and conversation is slowed to slightly less than racing speed. I receive no such consideration. At that time my French was equally basic, but my struggles to comprehend the missile-speed enquiries directed at me from all quarters, were merely treated as understandable bashfulness. Pleas to slow down were smilingly ignored. I was taught French from my earliest years in primary school by *une vraie Parisienne* and my accent has remained, even if the verb conjugations haven't. It can be a bit of a handicap at times.

Our host came up to introduce himself and treated my cheeks to the liveliest scrub they've had for many a year. He looked like a man still in mourning for Woodstock and wondering where the beautiful people are now. He was sporting a very fetching grey Afro, mismatched flip-flops and a three-day stubble. Despite appearances, he's actually a wealthy farmer from the fertile plains of the Lot et Garonne where, amongst other juicy delicacies they grow the best tomatoes in the world. We were informed that he comes back to this venerable house – where he was born – for one day only, the last Saturday in August every year, purely to give his traditional end-of-summer party for his friends and neighbours. Amazing.

We started with melon. Actually we started with seemingly limitless quantities of pastis, and woe betide us if we didn't watch the level in our glass; it refilled as if by magic, while we were desperately trying to understand what the hell our neighbours were waffling on about. A slightly less antique farm worker nudged me in the ribs and introduced himself through a lungful of smoke.

"Michel, *votre voisin*!" He intoned gruffly, and after lunging for a brief embrace began interrogating me about our moving plans. I thought I was bearing up remarkably well, until the sneezing began. Well, it was somewhere between a cough and a sneeze actually, clearly and puzzlingly directed at me.

"*Cooor*!" He ejaculated.

I smiled stupidly at him.

"*Cooor, cooor*!" He continued in frustration, his wagging cigarette alarmingly close to my bosom. "*Une semaine? Deux?*"

The *centime* dropped. He wanted to know when we were moving. *Quand*? I replied to the question, thankful that I'd got to the bottom of it. He nodded, muttered "*Ah bon*" several times and passed me a piece of melon. It was a large slice of juicy Quercynois that he'd thoughtfully hacked off for me with his penknife, and I don't think I have ever tasted a melon as cool and sweet; I don't think I've ever been less equipped to deal with one either. It dripped happily down my chin and onto my toes. Napkins, naturally, were out of the question, so I grabbed a handful of dried grass and went with the flow. After second helpings and some fastidious hand-wipings on a handy tea towel that some thoughtful soul had abandoned in a nearby oleander, I was beginning to get the hang of things and was quite ready for the second course. This was a traditional *soupe*, the rural sort that you find in many guises all over Europe. It generally consists of large pieces of country bread soaked in some sort of broth or stock. In France it's usually onion based and finished with whatever comes to hand, in summer it'll be tomatoes; it is fragrant, warming and remarkably filling, there began a mad scramble for bowls and, even rarer, spoons. My new neighbour shared his with me, which was extremely kind and I was fully conscious of the honour. We slurped away with gay abandon and I watched the end of his cigarette warily.

The wine was served next. It had arrived from two neighbouring vineyards in huge 50 litre plastic containers, with a tap. There was no shortage of glasses and soon everybody had one in hand. On with the food.

A gigantic tomato salad was presented in a plastic washing-up bowl. Dozens of sweet, juicy tomatoes, at the peak of ripeness, had been roughly hacked into pieces – no cheffy nonsense here – mixed with chopped anchovies and sliced olives then liberally doused with olive oil and vinegar. It was utterly delicious.

The beloved sidled up to me.

"Eat plenty, there may not be anything else," he warned gravely. I wasn't so sure, but as my salad bowl had already been re-filled twice by my attentive neighbour, it was somewhat academic. The bread came round again. Huge loaves of *pain de campagne*, the size of a Sussex trug, a single slice would cover a meat platter.

"Ah, la viande!" cried a huge bear of a man, disconcertingly resting one enormous paw on my shoulder. And sure enough the meat course had arrived, with some ceremony, in an orange box. Lamb or venison we were told, preferably both. He explained that a neighbouring farmer had donated the lamb and our host had shot the *biche*.

"In August?" I asked, a little surprised. He gave me a pitying look, proffered the box and confided,

"*Le congalateur, Madame*!" Of course. I gave my worried tummy a quick consoling rub and tried to take a small portion, it wasn't easy, all the small-looking pieces were actually joined to vast slices by a rubber sinew.

A spare chair materialised out of the murk, so I grabbed it, sat down and eyed a couple of the local curs, who knew instinctively – as dogs generally do – just who is most likely to provide the feast. I dropped a piece casually and took a nervous squint at my fellow guests. It was fully dark by this time, and ninety percent of the party were far too occupied to glance at me. The curs snaffled and growled. I smiled at my neighbour.

"Delicious!"

He got up and brought me another orange box, this time laden with chicken and *pintade* – guinea fowl – barbecued over an open fire. Served me right really.

In the next field the bonfire lit the night sky and the cicadas, which were providing the madrigal, reached a shrill crescendo. I sat back cradling my glass of wine and drank in the atmosphere. It was a beautiful, balmy evening, and although I was a trifle over-full, I had the satisfaction of knowing that I had acquitted myself with honour.

"Pizza!" Bellowed the bear as another course was passed out from the steps of the house. Surely not! But yes, there in yet another orange box, lay thirty or forty slices of rapidly cooling pizza. The bear located another spare chair and pulled it up beside me, his large hairy knee pressed firmly against mine. He sorted out the largest slice of pizza, and grinning triumphantly, plonked it on my plate. I shivered in panic; this was ridiculous, if I ate any more I'd be in need of first aid. The bear looked at me in concern, and then removing his greasy jumper he draped it round my shoulders, taking the opportunity to leer appreciatively down the front of my dress. Between my legs the curs jostled quietly for pole position, there was a pack of about six or seven around my chair by this time and they wolfed the pizza in seconds.

At that point there was a rustle, a few shouts and a faint scream from the trees on the far side of the bonfire.

"*Sanglier!*" A ravishing brunette, not a day over twelve, shot by in excitement, trailing local wide-boys. Things were getting a mite out of hand and I looked round, rather wildly, for my erstwhile protector. The man in question arrived about twenty minutes later to offer me another glass of wine.

"Enjoying it?" He asked brightly. He looked as if he'd been enjoying it thoroughly, and I wondered vaguely how the hell we were going to pick our way down the dark hillside, and whether or not there was any fear of him falling down a ravine in the process.

"You should come and see the house," he insisted, "there's an ancient stone *évier*, where they're doing the washing up, an old open fireplace, for the cooking, and that's it! No running water, electricity, or even bottled gas and no furniture at all. Mind you, there's a generator in that old barn for the lights."

'The lights' turned out to be one archaic spotlight that just about lit the wine-casks. I had presumed the bonfire in the nearby field was for barbequing purposes, but apparently not. The fire was for illumination, entertainment and general bonhomie only. The real business was conducted in a slightly – ever so slightly – more civilised manner, indoors.

Back in my inner circle, the cheese course had arrived. There was a choice of three local cheeses, Bleu des Causses, a rich, salty local blue, strong enough to take the roof off your mouth, a vast slice of a local Brebis, a pungent ewe's milk cheese, and a vast wedge of Cantal Vieux, which looked as if it had been recovered from Tutankhamun's tomb. They were served, naturally, from the ubiquitous orange boxes. I sliced a slender piece of Cantal and furtively dangled some of the bread down the side of my chair, nearly losing my fingers in the process.

Cheese is one of my great weaknesses but it loses its charms somewhat when you're already full to bursting and the only possible accompaniment is a vast slice of bread that would cover your knees. I took a wary bite. It was good. A slug of wine, it was really very good. The pack at my feet slavered in disappointment.

The bear leaned over to refill my glass and casually slid his massive arm round to join his jumper. Oh dear. I tried to edge away a little, and my thigh crashed into Michel, my sneezing neighbour, on the other side. He swivelled round, and with great courtesy gave me the benefit of his toothless grin, a bite of his Brebis and a gust of blue smoke. I smiled gamely and gave myself up for lost.

Meanwhile, at the other end of the clearing the dessert was beginning to make it's rounds. *Merveilles* are a truly delightful local delicacy, small, puffy, light cakes, flavoured with lemon or orange blossom water, drenched in sugar and very tasty. I took one – they're very small – and as the box passed on its way I made the huge mistake of expressing my delight at the subtle flavour, more were offered, and the bear wandered off to find a *tarte aux pruneaux,* just in case I was still a bit peckish. This wonderfully sticky comestible is made all round the area from the world famous *pruneaux d'Agen*. Having procured a vast cartwheel of it, the bear proceeded to hack it into rough wedges with Michel's penknife, offering me a triangular chunk the size of his two hands. Of course I had to refuse, delectable though I'm sure it would have been. I was packed into a communal circle tighter than an anchovy in a barrel, so there was absolutely no chance of slipping a bit to the faithful pack at my feet, and my distended stomach was in screaming uproar. It would be another six months before I could face a *tarte aux pruneaux* without flinching.

Fortunately, it was at this timely point in the proceedings that a frantically waving arm caught the corner of my eye; our guides were making 'shall we go' signs.

With profound relief I started to make my excuses to my new friends. Kisses were exchanged all round; cheeks were given a second scrubbing and somewhat rash invitations issued. I left them to enjoy the tart and the table full of dire-looking *digestifs* while I rounded up the children, deep in their own little group, and rooted out the beloved – who was contemplating yet another rendezvous with the wine tap.

"Watch out for snakes!" Grinned the bear and weaved back to attend to the eau-de-vie.

That was one wild night out we certainly won't forget in a hurry.

★ ★ ★

Le Quercy

This wild little corner of the world must surely be one of the most captivating spots in all France. Politically the northern part is now known as the Lot, bisected by the curvaceous river for which it was named and boasting ravishing scenery. The river used to be called Oltis – from the Latin – and was shortened to 'Olt' sometime in the following centuries and later still to the more pronounceable 'Lot'. You can still see the evidence everywhere along the banks in the names of villages such as St Vincent Rive D'Olt or the local wines, christened Cotes D'Olt. All along the river, west of Cahors the famous AOC vineyards of renowned *domaines* are artfully flung across the banks. Gilded by long days of sunshine to ripen the glistening grapes, and gifted with delicacies like *confits de canard, foie gras,* truffles and *cêpes*, plums, figs and walnuts, it's a gastronomic paradise. But I'm a little biased of course.

There are five distinct regions to this lovely place. Right on the northern boundary runs the Dordogne River, surrounded by beautifully preserved little bastide towns in a delightfully undulating landscape. It's a favourite with British holidaymakers; in fact when many people say they've been to the Dordogne, they've actually been in the Lot. Mind you, holidaymakers are not the only ones to have made this classic error. In her seminal and gargantuan work, French Provincial Cooking, Elizabeth David made a similar mistake. The Perigord is the old name for the Dordogne departement; it doesn't encompass the Quercy. The towns of Souillac, Moissac, Capdenac and Figeac are in the Quercy. The river Lot also runs through the Quercy and doesn't go anywhere near the Perigord – and neither does the mighty Garonne. Sorry Elizabeth, we are all infinitely indebted to you for pulling the scales from our eyes and training our palates, but your geography may have been a trifle faulty. Having got that off my chest let me continue. To the northwest the gentle Bouriane is a softer landscape, charming golden stone villages in rolling countryside. To the northeast, the Causses du Quercy are high windswept plains, a rugged wilderness of outstanding beauty, spattered with sheep and goats, and home to Rocamadour, the most famous shrine in this part of France. It is in effect the tail end of the Massif Central and the whole area is now officially a national park. To the southeast lie the Causse de Limogne and the Quercy Rouergue. Not quite as untamed but equally beautiful, full of sheer cliffs containing prehistoric troglodyte caves and precariously perched fortified villages. If you visit the area you simply must stop to look at the famous, 20,000 year old cave paintings in the echoing caverns of Pech Merle, conclusive proof that this area has been continuously inhabited for far longer than recorded history might suggest. It's an astounding place.

Then, if you turn west you'll find the landscape beginning to flatten slightly, into the blazing fields and vineyards that lie in my favourite bit of all – of course, in this, I'm outrageously biased – the lovely southwest. The cliffs that rear either side of the road are bone white, radiating heat. Farmhouses are now a very pale grey, bleached almost white in the glaring sun. This is the Quercy Blanc, named for the white stone that makes up the landscape and litters the fields. Vineyards are draped enticingly over the more gentle rises, lavender, santolina and holm oak cling to rocky outcrops and the sun is hot on your bare skin. Not just warm, hot.

It's an old region, and in ancient times extended very much further south, beyond the city of Montauban to the southern limits of what is now the Tarn et Garonne – named for obvious reasons. However the land itself is still widely known by its original title. From the undulating Dordogne to the mighty Garonne as long as anyone can remember it's been known as Le Quercy and as far as the locals are concerned it always will be. If you glance at a map you'll see dozens of little villages with the suffix en Quercy, defiantly underlining their heritage. Having said that, it has to be admitted that the reason for the name is a bone of some contention.

A few learned historians declare the whole area was named for the numerous oak forests that romp across the hills, again derived from the Latin quercus – oak. This seems like a highly plausible explanation, until you delve a little further back and discover that the claims of others may well have some substance, quite a lot of substance. They maintain that the area was named for the ancient 'Cadurci', the indigenous tribe that once peopled the province and founded the city of Cahors around the 8th century BC. Roughly the same period in history that another insignificant – but ambitious – tribe were founding their little city in the Tiber valley of central Italy. Then just a little further west, the great Byzas was laying the foundations for his fabulous cosmopolitan city on the heights of Pera along the beautiful, blue shores of the Bosphorus. The Cadurciens were in rich and illustrious company, and I'm personally inclined to believe that it was they who named the town. The current inhabitants agree. A native of Cahors is still called a Cadurcien, and it's a coveted title.

Of course it's entirely possible there have been so many composites of the name over the millennia that the truth will remain forever shrouded in the mists of time, but one thing is quite certain, this place has been called Quercy for a long time and it isn't going to change now.

*

Beautiful Cahors is a diminutive city with a population of only 20,000, boasting layer upon layer of history. It is a partly Roman, partly medieval, slightly renaissance and partly nineteenth century town, famed for its powerful black wines – much favoured by the ancient Popes and Russian Tsars – its seven hundred year old bridge, its lively markets and fabulous little restaurants. The city was built in a great loop of the river and is surrounded on all sides by the looming hills, making it much more defensible in days of yore, and much less susceptible to sprawling development now. For many hundreds of years there were actually a highly extravagant three bridges, a trifle unnecessary considering the amount of traffic on the roads in such times. Sadly they're no longer standing, but you can still see the sunken traces of one, just up river from the comparatively modern Pont Louis-Philippe. It was Roman like the city they ruthlessly occupied and which with true Roman arrogance they renamed, Divona Cadurcorum. But of all the bridges that ever-graced Cahors, the most illustrious by far is the fourteenth century Pont Valentré, a medieval masterpiece that, luckily for us, is still standing. More than that, it's recently been totally restored, rather over-restored in my opinion. When I first saw it as a wondering child, the massive form was so unsafe I wasn't allowed near it. Nobody could cross it then. Now its once crumbling stonework has been dressed or replaced and pointed to perfection. The famous silhouette stands proud once more and in sharp contrast to the various liquid blues of river and sky. It is currently celebrating its 700th birthday, a pretty decent age – even for a bridge – and is again open to public use, on foot only. It has also recently been endowed with World Heritage Site status and now graces a million wine bottles and countless million postcards, many of which recount the famous legend:

It is said that the architect, frustrated by the slow progress of construction work – the bridge took more than half a century to build - sold his soul to the devil in exchange for assistance. When the masonry was almost complete and the architect was beginning to feel the weight of years, he tried to back out of the deal by ordering the devil to carry water to the site in a sieve, enraging the fiery soul. This was possibly not the smartest of moves. In revenge the devil removed the final stone of the final tower each night and threw it into the river below. Every day the long-suffering masons replaced it, only to be thwarted again the following night. The devil still clings to the central tower; carved in stone, so if you plan to walk across the cobbled span of the patriarch of bridges – especially after dark – do be careful!

This enchanting old town fascinates me, and although I'm in and out several times a week I am always there on a Wednesday morning; market day. There's a daily market in the covered *halles*, and a twice-weekly market – Wednesday and Saturday – in the Place Jean-Jacques Chapou, right by the early gothic, double domed cathedral of St. Etienne, a treasured national monument. Of course Saturday here is like Saturday in any city centre anywhere else in the world, thoroughly over-crowded. The Wednesday market is a little quieter, a little more local and much more to my liking.

I generally start marketing expeditions from the south side

and walk past the *halles* where the stalls are not only covered but permanent. Here you can buy all the essentials on any day of the week. There's even a stall selling Cahors wine *en vrac*, loose, the way almost all locals will buy it if they don't happen to have a vineyard themselves, or know a man who does. I wander on past the old lady selling soaps and lotions made from local lavender and olive oil and past the sausage man on the corner. He's young, jaunty and dressed for the tourists in a blue and white striped matelot t-shirt, a short white apron and black beret. His delicious stall is one of the prettiest in the market, festooned with every conceivable variety of *saucisson sèche,* from *sanglier* to *noix* to the ordinary, everyday pork. I squeeze past admiring Americans with oversized cameras and carrying voices, and plunge straight into the humming mêlée of a truly competitive market.

Stallholders lure me with slivers of *fromage de brebis* – which I ignore with a smile and a nod – a dozen different types of goat's cheese or a free *merveille*, fresh from the oven. I try hard to stick to my shopping list, but it's not at all easy, temptation is absolutely everywhere. I invariably come away with my basket overflowing. In spring it's stuffed with fresh greens, rape and *points de chou* – the local answer to purple sprouting broccoli – herbs and pungent bunches of what look for all the world like red spring onions, but are in fact, *aillet*, young spring garlic. I always pause at the cheapest vegetable stall, thickly surrounded by local ladies, where there's generally a pantomime performance in full flow. In winter there are serious discussions on the merits of the late winter leeks with the enthusiastic stallholder.

"Slender and white as a mermaid's arms, sweet as her kisses," he grins at one of his elderly clients. "*Deux kilos, jeune Mademoiselle?*" She cackles delightedly and nods in flattered acquiescence. I smile and move on to one of my favourite little stalls, right by the walls of the cathedral. The old lady who presides here is always besieged. Her homegrown produce is cheap and well presented. I have to stand patiently in line, while she twinkles about in her pinny and zip-up slippers. I will buy half a dozen eggs straight from the farmyard and half a yard of local sausage, then succumb to a huge Savoy cabbage that I don't need and can't fit in the basket anyway. I can make a *chou farci*, I'll tell myself consolingly. Perhaps I'll buy four fresh discs of *cabecou* from the goat's cheese stall in the central aisle, then I'll make my escape before things get totally out of hand, and I'm off to the *boulangerie*.

Later in the year the produce changes completely. There are perfumed peaches warm from the sun and vast red peppers. Red mullet from the Mediterranean, towering mounds of slender *haricots vert*, glorious, juicy tomatoes from Marmande, huge bunches of basil, exquisite – and totally unnecessary – armfuls of cloudy linaria and colourful statice. As I shop on a weekday, and as long as I remember to time my marketing to end well before noon, I'm pretty certain to find spare chairs outside my favourite café, where I collapse and enjoy a leisurely *café crème* or *Perrier menthe*.

In the bad old days the noisy RN20 used to run straight through the heart of the old city. You were just as likely to come across a shoal of caravans struggling along, desperate for a sniff of the sea, or an articulated monstrosity belching out lead and monoxide, as a local on his bike, daily bread strapped to his back. Not any more, Cahors has a bypass now, and to be fair, it's worth taking this route at least once, just for the panoramic view of the city from the Viaduc de Roquebilière.

But the best way to really get to the heart of the old town is without doubt to drive – or better still to walk – straight down the centre and into the lovely Boulevard de Gambetta, named for Léon, sometime premier of France, architect of the third republic and one of Cahors' most famous sons, born here in 1838. The road is lined with tall renaissance buildings and statuesque plane trees. To the east they're backed with the narrow, winding remains of the original city – medieval buildings on Roman foundations – to the west the newer, more practical buildings, such as the hospital and post office, railway station and *préfecture*. On the boulevard itself dozens of cafés and captivating little shops stand back to allow an illusion of space. They're interspersed with the grander buildings, the cathedral, *Hotel de Ville* and *Palais de Justice*. It all adds up to a delightful *mélange* of old and not so old, a humming, charming place.

The boulevard is actually a relatively new addition to the many-layered tapestry of this ancient place. It was constructed only a few hundred years ago when the old fortified ditch was removed, which is why it's guarded at one end by the old city barbican and at the other by a huge fountain and the river. It's also the reason that all the medieval streets are to be found to the east of the town. A vast tangle of narrow, cobbled lanes, shadowed and quiet, their ancient sites dictated by the Cadurciens, their memories stretching back to before the birth of Christ. One of my favourite little squares is the Place de St Urcisse, just round the corner from the church of the same name, one of the oldest in Cahors, resting on stones that certainly predate the Christians who built it. Restaurants jostle cheek by jowl here and the preserved medieval facades of the houses are so aesthetically pleasing that I always find myself emerging onto the nearby riverside walk with a distinct crick in my neck from too much looking up. I like to walk back down river from there, to the fountain and gardens at the foot of the Pont Louis-Philippe. Perhaps a little picnic with a warm baguette from the bakery on the boulevard and a fresh Rocamadour cheese from the market, maybe a few cherry tomatoes and a Perrier. Bliss. I'll then have the strength for the not-too-difficult walk around the loop in the river to the symbol of the town.

Despite its devilish reputation, the majestic Pont Valentré was an accepted and essential part of one of the most famous of all pilgrim trails, the trek to Santiago de Compostella, where the apostle St. James is supposedly buried. It's still a much used trail, mainly for hikers nowadays, but you do see the odd few sporting the ancient symbol of the saint himself, used by all penitents on this pilgrimage, the scallop shell, hence its French name, *coquille de Saint Jacques*.

From the bridge, you can walk straight up into the centre of town - past the excavations where body-pierced young archaeologists are uncovering layer upon layer of social history, along the Allées Fenelon, named for another famous son of the city, and into the charming central place. This is where the great man himself presides, in his bronze persona, and where my favourite café spills out over the square. It's also where I'm generally to be found more than ready for a delightful lunch, late on a Wednesday morning.

As I plump down into a sun-soaked chair, the short-sleeved waiter glides over and grabs my hand. Occasionally he'll risk a ritual kiss, which always flummoxes me – strait-laced English girl that I am – and asks,

"Ca va Madame? Un grand crème ou le menu?"

I feel a warm glow that he regards me as one of his regulars, proud to belong.

I could easily linger there for a couple of hours, listening to the burble of the fountains, watching the sun playing on the ancient clock tower and admiring the perfect contrast the old stone makes with the cerulean smudge of sky. How many millions have done the same over the past two thousand years, I wonder?

Beautiful, timeworn Cahors, there's an irresistible pull to it.

* * *

A Ham-Fisted Attempt At Nöel

The long hot summer finally seemed to be over; gentle autumn was passing and the few golden leaves still clinging tenaciously to the vines were just waiting for the first frosts. We awoke one morning in late November to find that winter had arrived in the Quercy, and in some style. The valley below shivered like a bride under a veil of glittering white; our last few garden crops lay prostrate on the ground and the indoor temperatures made us hop around on the freezing tiles as if we were walking on ice.

The beloved disappeared into the kitchen to poke and cajole Cruella – our wood-burning stove is a Deville and her name was a foregone conclusion – into a little more effort, whilst I donned layers of T-shirts and all the spare jumpers I possessed. Opening the back door twenty minutes later, to grab an extra couple of logs, my eyes popped open and the ready exclamation very nearly escaped my tightly buttoned lip.

It was six degrees below zero. Quite obviously it was time

to turn our attention to indoor activities, activities like the Christmas cooking.

Christmas and the winter equinox have always been a time of feasting in Europe, no matter where you happen to be. In France, of course, feasting of any description is a national obsession and a month or so before the winter festive season vast quantities of assorted meats in various stages of preparation begin to appear.

For quite a little while I'd been meaning to have a bash at my own ham. I don't mean just boiling a bit of cellophane-wrapped, pre-brined stuff from the supermarket shelves. I'm referring to the age-old practice of turning an immense and unwieldy leg of pork into a splendid baked ham. It isn't as easy as it sounds. Firstly you have to find your leg. Assuming you don't have a farm, and therefore no animal to donate the required piece of meat, you will have to buy it. You'd think this would be a pretty straightforward exercise but in fact on this occasion it turned out to be more than a little complicated. The time to buy good pork in rural France is in late autumn, from about the middle of October to the end of November. The market stalls; *boucheries* and even the supermarkets are stuffed with it. They have *foires de porc* and sausage weeks, meat deals and promotions galore.

Whilst I was tentatively buying a small *roti* from the excellent and suitably portly butcher in my local supermarket, I was somewhat distracted by a little old lady rummaging determinedly in the chilled cabinet. I watched in awe as she stocked her trolley with two *jambons* of pork, a huge length of chops – still attached and therefore about three feet long, followed by about fifty feet of Toulouse sausage. You could have scaled the peaks of the Pyrenees with it, then built a fire and fed several companies of scouts. God knows what she was going to do with it all.

This porky fling lasted for about six weeks and then, just as I was really beginning to get into the spirit of the thing, it was over. The offers were gone; attention had turned to *foie gras* and all things duck and goose. Nobody had a leg of pork to spare. This was a trifle disconcerting as by this time I'd more or less made up my mind that this was definitely the year to do it.

"I want a leg of pork." I informed the beloved.

"For Christmas?" he asked, his eyes still glued to his precious computer screen.I explained patiently that given the choice I would prefer a small gift-wrapped cadeau from Cartier or Chanel for my surprise gift, as a leg of pork might conceivably create a ladder in my Christmas stocking. I was, however, desirous of acquiring the afore-mentioned item for gastronomic purposes. He grunted absently.

"I think we should salt our own ham this year", I offered encouragingly, "and it's past time to get it into the brine".

So it was agreed – a little reluctantly I think – that we should go on a pork hunt that afternoon. Needless to say, there wasn't a leg to be had anywhere in the Quercy. I couldn't believe it; only a few days earlier they'd been absolutely everywhere. After an exhausting afternoon, we finally ran one to ground in the well-patronised *boucherie* of a local village. The only problem was its extreme bulk; the donor must have been a porker the size of a rhinoceros. Naturally, after a whole afternoon of searching, I wasn't going to mention this minor detail, but I couldn't help wondering whether I might yet be reduced to boiling it in the old iron bath we'd found at the bottom of the garden. We transported our carefully wrapped purchase home and installed it in the kitchen sink, where I stood for quite a few minutes gloating over the prize and wondering just what the hell to do next. In the end I did what I always do in moments of culinary uncertainty. I consulted a good book. In this case it was the excellent 'Charcuterie and

French Pork Cookery' a forty-year-old seminal work by the late and much missed Jane Grigson. I then raked out a more up-to-date tome; Hugh Fearnley-Whittingstall's 'River Cottage Cook Book', Hugh gives precise instructions for ladies in just my kind of dilemma. He also warns about the necessity of ensuring that one's pans and ovens are large enough for the enterprise before embarking on it. Sage Counsel. Tucking Jane under one arm, I squeezed Hugh rather less comfortably under the other and prepared for battle.

I dithered for an hour or so whilst raking out the required salt, sugar, white wine, bay leaves and peppercorns, then spent another freezing fifteen minutes head-down in a prickly hedgerow gathering the accursed juniper berries, after which I tried lowering the beast into my largest preserving pan. It didn't fit.

I ground my teeth and decided to retire for a bath, using the rather more sophisticated apparatus in my bathroom I hasten to add, for purposes of relaxation and divine enlightenment. This often works for me, I usually find that if I'm going to have a eureka moment it's more often than not in the bath. Hardly surprising of course, but I like to enhance the possibility of a brainwave by filling the bath with fragrant, steamy bubbles, to relax both mind and body, and taking a large glass of good red wine with me to lubricate the thought processes. It rarely fails. Anyway, whatever forces were in the ascendancy, they certainly worked that time. The solution of course was blindingly simple. I cut the leg in half. This gave me two good size hams of five and a half kilos. Naturally the 'cutting' was a bit of a pantomime and involved a fair bit of dancing around the problem with sharpened knives and small saws, but in the end it was relatively easy.

Meanwhile, in the drawing room the two children were delving into vast cardboard Christmas decoration boxes, hauled down from the attics that morning. Screams of delight reached my ears as they uncovered the moth-eaten nativity scene that had adorned the mantelpiece for the past fifteen years.

"We three Kings from Orient are..." bawled my son, tunelessly, hauling out yards of half-bald tinsel. "Can I have this in my room?" I acquiesced gladly. His sudden musical outburst reminded me of my own childhood. Whilst bellowing out this particular carol, I honestly thought we were singing about a petrol station. In France at that time there was a chain called AnTar, and I presumed they were akin. Three Kings? Well sort of oil-rich Arab sheiks I supposed. After all, the Magi came from the east didn't they? It seemed perfectly obvious to me.

Anyway, back to the ham! On Cruella's hob, I had a vast pan of brine ingredients slowly – very slowly – thinking about coming to a boil.

A ham has to be soaked in brine for three or four weeks, depending on its size. Now that I had two smaller hams to deal with, three weeks would be sufficient. This was a relief in itself, as the hams were intended to feed the myriad visitors at Christmas, which by this time was only three weeks away.

The beloved had decided, in his infinite wisdom, that the only possible receptacle for this endeavour was a plastic box with a lid, issued some time ago by a well-known UK supermarket chain. I gave it a good scrub with a dubious looking product that smelled strongly of bleach and put it outside on the covered terrace, with the pork carefully wedged inside to await the brine. We had decided on the terrace as a suitable place for storage after realising, with a bit of a jolt, that the fridge was nowhere near large enough to accommodate our prize, and that a temperature of less than five degrees was crucial to the success of the enterprise. Fortunately winter weather in this part of France is cold, crisp and sunny. Temperatures are considerably colder than in England, making a short-term outside storage system a viable alternative. It occurred to me that if I was going to leave a feast on the doorstep, some sort of anti-visiting-dog device might be a prudent precaution, so I heaved a large piece of Quercy stone and a small potted olive tree on top and retired to attend to the supper.

Next morning the brine ingredients had done their job and amalgamated beautifully. The beloved put the brine outside to cool a little more whilst we breakfasted. After a few slices of toasted baguette, splendidly crisped by Cruella, I flexed my muscles and continued with the job in hand. It was just possible, I mulled reflectively, that as the piggy part of this fusion process weighed a good eleven kilos and the brine was a good fifteen litres, the whole might be beyond my strength to lift. This unsurprisingly proved to be the case. One thing was certain, once lodged on the terrace, my hams weren't going anywhere. I sloshed the murky brown liquid into the accommodating box and added a few more bay leaves for luck, then I lowered my specimens into their marinade. Of course as there were umpteen kilos of salt in the mixture the hams floated like rubber ducks in a baby bath. I grabbed a couple of bowls, balanced them on top of the meat and rammed the lid down. The beloved huffed, puffed, staggered and heaved the thing out onto the terrace where I carefully replaced the stone.

One Quercy ham, pickled.

*

The next item on my Christmas feasting list was the quintessential southwestern bird. A nice fat Toulouse goose.

The French translation of goose is '*oie*' – an odd looking word – and surprisingly one that, up to now, I'd had no call to use. As we drove to the market to enquire about reserving a bird, the beloved and I had the most bizarre conversation.

"How do you pronounce it then?" He asked casually.

I gave this a little consideration. "I'm not absolutely certain. I suppose… I cogitated, I suppose it's an… *oy*."

He chewed on that for a minute or two.

"But if you think about the pronunciation of *foie* …" He let the suggestion hang.

"You mean you think it's a *wa*?" I asked. *Oy* was ridiculous enough, but *wa*! Could I really enquire at the *boucherie* if the time was right for ordering a Christmas… *wa*! We finally resolved the issue by raking out the battered copy of Larousse kept permanently in the glove box for just such emergencies. And of course it is a *wa*.

In the market I hopped around the likeliest stall, admiring the beribboned birds and trying to look knowledgeable. The stallholder wasn't taken in for a minute.

"Oui Madame?"

Damn, damn, damn! I stitched a weak smile onto my face and enquired about a possible… *wa?*

"*Les oies?*" Actually what he said was '*Lezeoohah?*' He went on to explain that I could certainly have one but not until Christmas Eve, and only then if I ordered in advance. Now would be the ideal time, how large would I like it?

So that was that. I ordered my Christmas feast, a large goose, without the prized and expensive liver, and had the order repeated back to me in correct local patois.

"*Unagrandewasonnefwa*" Well quite.

*

A few weeks after my hammy high jinks we were invited to our neighbour's house for New Year aperitifs. We were to arrive at

12.30 on a Sunday afternoon – which meant at least half an hour later as naturally nobody ever arrives on time in France. We were looking forward to this encounter, but with some trepidation, as our neighbours spoke absolutely no English. This was fair enough of course and, on its own, we would have been able to cope with it quite well, but they added to this minor hurdle by having extremely strong southwestern accents. This meant that when confronted with a polite

'*Ca va*?' They were likely to reply,

'*Tribyanga*!' or even more confusingly '*engfohma*!' Which can complicate matters a trifle.

However, on the appointed day we spruced ourselves up a bit and after a short discussion on whether or not a dictionary would be a socially acceptable accessory – opinion was split, so we left it behind – set off, resolutely determined to prove that the English were as linguistically talented as any other nation in Europe. Hmmm.

We arrived to a great show of bonhomie, dozens of smacking kisses, a five-minute rocket-fired greeting, of which I managed to catch about one word in ten, and a rash of very dubious looking bottles. We concentrated fiercely, simultaneously translating dialect into French and French into English then smiling inanely when our mental computers refused to co-operate. André, our enthusiastic host, encouraged by our apparent comprehension, put a foot hard down and revved up the speed of his conversation like a turbo-charged Michael Schumacher. Huge drinks were thrust into our hands and refilled whenever we weren't paying close attention. Salty little snacks circulated, olives, pickled chillies *maison* and spiced cornichons followed. It was going to be one of those days.

An hour or so later we stood, somewhat dazed, on the sun-drenched terrace with our host. He had slowed his conversation a little at this stage to allow him to cope more effectively with the vast pastis in his hand. It was obviously time to start making 'time to go – lunch in the oven' type noises and we were just congratulating ourselves on our successful emergence from this linguistic assault course when Francine popped her head round the long windows. Would we care to eat with them? The beloved propped himself against the stone wall for support whilst I stammered an inarticulate, wholly inaccurate and completely untruthful reply.

"*C'est trés simple*" she assured us.

We began with two different varieties of *pâté maison.* There were coarse *rillettes* made from the local wild boar – the famed *sanglier* of the dense forests here – and there was a vast terrine of everyday pork *pâté.* These were served with the same sort of *pain de campagne* that we'd experienced during our unforgettable 'orange box' barbeque some months before. Large portions were encouraged and second helpings were obligatory. The first jug of local Cahors, made by our host's brothers further down the valley, was finished and smoothly replaced with another. This was followed by another of the house specialities; stuffed neck of duck, roasted crisply and served with vast quantities of *haricots vert* and another jug of Cahors. It was delectable. I sat back and tried to recoup what little strength I had left, whilst our host, having partly satisfied his nutritional requirements and virtually drowned his tonsils, was back to full speed anecdotes. Francine appeared with a tray of succulent, ripe cheeses and another basket of foot long slices of bread. André's exuberant non-stop conversation was causing the onboard computer between my ears to signal overload. My stomach had given up signalling and was now quietly grumbling away to itself. The beloved, however, was still manfully ploughing on. His third helping of Vigny cheese necessitated yet another jug of Cahors to which he applied himself, I thought, with admirable dedication. Our hostess slipped away to bring on the triumph of the meal, *gateau pastis quercynois*, another very local and ridiculously filling speciality. I wondered whether the amiable dog of the house was within my reach. The last drop of Cahors was shared out and a bottle of Champagne appeared. Wine glasses were replaced with more appropriately shaped flutes and the *gâteau* ceremoniously cut. I accepted my portion with every evidence of delight and as we toasted the New Year, I slipped it quietly into my capacious jacket pocket. André polished off his first slice with relish, and having cut himself another, went in search of the most dubious bottle of all. He tried to explain just how this highly acclaimed *digestif* was made, by brandishing the herbs in front of us. Artemisia, the name rang a bell on the edge of my sozzled consciousness. André poured a small quantity – which was unlike him – and I suddenly made the connection. Of course, Artemisia or wormwood, it was absinthe! No wonder the quantities were small. At this point the grandfather clock in the corner began to make wheezing, getting-ready-to-strike sounds. We glanced up. It was six o'clock. Having thanked our hosts for a glorious '*trés simple*' lunch, we heaved our bloated bodies out of their chairs and staggered home. The simple aperitif had turned into a five-course, five-hour marathon. The *épaule d'agneau* I had originally intended for our lunch stood forlornly on the kitchen worktop. Anyone for dinner?

★

'We owe three dinner parties.' The beloved informed me suddenly. It was the morning after the prolonged aperitifs and we were breakfasting on coffee and kaolin. I was a little startled by this confident pronouncement and asked him if he was sure. It's unlike the beloved to keep track of such things, and this was the second time in six months that he'd suggested a dinner party.

Life in France was having an unexpected socialising effect on him. He nodded and swallowed another teaspoon of kaolin.

'Francine and André, Alicia and Michael, Hélène and Francois.'

I chewed on this thought for a moment. He was right. I fished out the diary and we discussed possible dates. It gave me the perfect excuse for another little gastronomic journey that I'd been keen to take for a little while – when the opportunity arose – developing a recipe for my own *pâté maison.*

Making a pork-based *pâté*, or if you want to be a little more posh, a terrine, is a relatively simple affair. Masses of pork, flavoured with a little liver or game and some sort of alcohol, along with the ubiquitous garlic and a goodly sprinkling of fresh herbs. There are three fundamental ways to go about the business. You can make a straightforward *pâté*, all the same all the way through. You can layer it with different meats and turn it into what the English call a terrine. Or you can make what the Quercynois regard as the real thing; a vast quantity of *pâté* cooked in an old earthenware dish, usually oval, always high-sided and the origin of the term now used for the posh versions. The first two are always turned out and evenly sliced and they look very beautiful indeed when served with a little salad. The last can be turned out or left in, as you prefer. Most country *charcuteries* and all the auberges in the Quercy opt for the latter. It's easier to keep, easier to wrap and it looks very authentic as the centrepiece of a large buffet table.

I decided on the first option. I wanted to serve it in slices with salad and besides, my smallest terrine would hold enough *pâté* to feed a Roman legion. I raked out the main ingredient. A whopping piece of pork from some unlikely part of the pig, along with a precious piece of hard back fat. A little liver came next. As luck would have it I happened to have some tender lamb's liver from the scrubland around the venerable town of Gramat in the high Causses. A handful or so of the stale breadcrumbs from yesterday's baguette, and possibly an egg, would create the necessary binding. A few cloves of garlic, a few peppercorns and a few juniper berries, from the bushes growing wild all over the hillsides around here, would supply extra flavour. For the herby part of the concoction I'd need a couple of handfuls of fresh parsley and another of rosemary from the rock-lined herb garden below the kitchen window. I flirted briefly with the idea of lining the tin with streaky bacon; it looks wonderfully professional when you turn it out and it does protect the *pâté*, but it is a bit arty-farty and I didn't have any, so that solved that one. The splendid salt from L'Adour river flats at Bayonne was next on the list, a good slosh of Armagnac and another of Cahors wine.

I stood back to survey the spread and decided that should just about do it. Now all I had to do was turn it all into a *pâté*.

Ten minutes later I had a perfect *pâté* consistency and looked as if I'd just emerged from a particularly bloody bullfight. My two-pound/one-kilo loaf tin just about held the enormous mixture. I pressed it down, covered it in kitchen foil and slipped it into a large Bain Marie, then into Cruella, who valiantly held a (roughly) 170-degree temperature, for just under two hours. No mean feat for a wood burning stove. Just time for me to enjoy a glass of wine and a relaxing bath, I felt I needed both.

Two hours later I raked the results of my endeavour out of the oven, it looked beautiful. I tested it for heat, admired it from all sides and topped it with a foil wrapped hunk of rock for compression and to facilitate slicing.

Outside there was a growl of over-excited car engine and I could see lights in our lane. Our neighbours' eldest son and his extremely beautiful girlfriend had parked their dilapidated, but highly embellished Renault outside the house, and were now busy ringing in the New Year on each other's tonsils. I raised a glass of wine to them and slid the *pâté* out of the window onto the sill.

The next morning I could hardly contain my excitement. I know, I know; it's really very sad, but there you are, I was excited. I removed the rock, eased the *pâté* away from the sides of the tin and turned it out onto my emerald green meat plate. I had no idea what it would taste like, but it looked divine.

There was a woeful woof by the back door as that same neighbour's friendly, waggy and incurably greedy golden Labrador announced her presence.

"Wow!" The beloved remarked approvingly, wandering in right on cue, hair wet from the shower, clutching a small flannel to protect his modesty. The back door burst open and thirty kilos of ravenous dog bounced in. Her face was covered from nose to ears in sticky black mud. Batman in a blonde fur coat. My hero sprang to the rescue, but as his only form of defence was a small flannel that I judged to be rather better employed where it was, he wasn't a great deal of assistance. I ushered him out of the room with stern orders to put his trousers on, and tried to push an understandably reluctant hound back outside. She stubbornly dug in all four paws and refused to budge. Unfortunately for her our kitchen floor is tiled in glazed terracotta and traction isn't easy. I heaved at her hind end – still wagging in a desperate attempt to ingratiate herself and change my mind – and she slid grudgingly back out onto the terrace. I shut the door firmly and went back to gaze at my *pâté*. It really hadn't been at all difficult but it gave a satisfying and no doubt wholly undeserved sense of achievement.

A toast to the pig.

★ ★ ★

Cities of Rose Brick, Grey Stone and Sacred Rock
Toulouse, Figeac and Rocamadour

"You've never been to Toulouse?" My neighbours were shocked at my pathetic ignorance of this glittering city. I explained that my experiences had hitherto been limited to Blagnac airport and the ring road. Hélène threw up her hands in horror and turned to study her schedule.

"You must go, at once. I will come with you, next Friday. Shopping! *Oui?"* She swivelled her ample hips to demonstrate the irresistible opportunities of a good girls' day out. It sounded like my kind of thing and I hurried indoors to check that the precarious state of the finances would stand the extra strain.

Two weeks later we were bombing down the autoroute at God-only-knew what speed; we certainly had no idea because the speedo in the ancient Renault was broken. The weather was absolutely foul too. After weeks of constant sunshine and blue skies, we were now subjected to sheets of grey rain that you could hardly see through. Hélène swerved to avoid an articulated giant and hooted at another. I offered up a silent prayer and hung on to my seat, the little white tin can we were travelling in seemed a trifle flimsy and inadequate in these atrocious conditions. Amazingly we did manage to reach Toulouse more or less intact. After many months of negotiating Cahors, and certainly after two hours of motorway driving with Hélène, I'd thought I was becoming quite used to French driving, but the huge intersections in the centre of this lively city were quite outside my experience. Cars faced in every conceivable direction, hooting, swerving and edging forward, the occupants leaning out of open windows furiously waving with one hand and removing the other from the steering wheel to adjust their cigarettes, run their hair back into place or even execute a smouldering embrace. Students on bikes wobbled precariously between them all, and the shuttle buses blocked everyone's view. I put my hands over my eyes until we had safely parked in one of the vast subterranean car parks. As we emerged from the frighteningly cranky lifts, the rain stopped, the clouds rolled away and we stepped into brilliant sunlight in the beautiful Place du Capitole, and what a magnificent sight it was.

One side of this enormous square is taken up with the vast, sumptuous *Hotel de Ville*. Built of marble and the local pink stone that has given the city its charming sobriquet, *la cité rose*, this is a massive, ornate building. You can walk straight through the centre of it, past marble statues and inner courtyards overflowing with immaculately tended flowers and studded with potted fig and olive trees. Being France, the other three sides of the place are naturally lined with inviting street cafés. We decided to stop for a little refreshment and I ordered my usual *grand crème*, to Hélène's evident disgust. Who would be seen drinking those great brown things? She told me severely that her sons had stopped drinking milk at the age of six – probably wouldn't dare do anything else I thought rebelliously – I smiled vaguely and asked her what she would like.

"A *Montalo* " she told me.

"A what?"

"*Montalo, Montalo* – it's quite common. Just ask him for a *Montalo*." I did as I was told – one tends to with Hélène, she's a schoolteacher – and two minutes later both the despised *grand crème* and the *Montalo* arrived. And of course it was a *menthe à l'eau*. I made a mental note to brush up on my café speak.

After the coffee, came the serious businesses of shopping and showing-off, two pastimes at which the French excel. We toured the centre, stopping at the wonderful Musée Paul Dupuy to examine the current exhibits and rest our aching feet. We toured the bookshops, the clothes shops, the shoe shops, the *patisseries*, the chocolate shops and the *magasin de savon de violettes*, a local speciality. The streets are narrow, medieval and cobbled in places. They are also slightly tilted to the centre, to help sewage run away in days of old and help rainwater run away now. Some of the buildings are so tall and so heavily shuttered they give the streets a dark, almost sinister feel. You're reminded that the Cathars were around here a few hundred years before you. There are no grisly exhibits and monstrous instruments of torture as there are in Carcassonne, but once away from the crowded centre and into the back streets you can still feel the heavy presence of fear that those dark times engendered.

As the streets widen, the houses become more ornate, some buildings are heavily timbered, whilst others are built totally of stone, and even more are built of the famous rose brick that the wealthy merchants adored. They are all quite beautiful, and my neck began to ache from craning upwards.

We paused for an infusion of caffeine – without milk – partly because I was too much of a wimp to insist, and partly because I felt that if I was going to live and work in France I really should start to drink my coffee normal, at least in public and especially in company.

This beautiful town was founded over two thousand years ago by an ancient tribe known as the Voques Tectosages. Then it was inevitably taken over by the acquisitive Romans, who immediately realised its strategic position, situated as it is between the thriving ports of the Mediterranean and the equally successful ports of the Atlantic, and positioned right on the Garonne River. Eventually the Canal du Midi was built to take full advantage of these natural assets and cut out the necessary trade routes from the Mediterranean, through the straits of Gibraltar and along the pirate strewn Spanish coast. Of course nowadays the lovely canal is a tourist trap, which is a bit of a shame, but the same cannot be said of dynamic Toulouse. It continues to push out into new industries, even now. The Cité d'Espace is represented by a huge, shining model of the European space shuttle, Ariane, which you can admire from the ring road as you head south to the sea. This is the birthplace, and the final resting place, of Concorde, perhaps the greatest, and without doubt the most elegant, passenger aircraft ever built. It's also the home of the European giant, Airbus and its new super-craft – which looks to me like a blue whale – but I still mourn the passing of Concorde, so I'm a little biased. It seems this place is vying with its American counterpart for the supremacy.

In contrast, the old part of the city, where Hélène and I had gathered our blisters, is paved with medieval splendour and gilded with all the graciousness and excess of the fifteenth, sixteenth and seventeenth centuries, when the immense power of the Comtes de Toulouse – almost all christened Raymond, just to confuse later generations – rivalled that of the throne. They were of royal extraction and could trace their lineage back, through Guilhelm de Toulouse, to the Merovingian Kings. There are even those who claim that the Toulousain line can be traced back to Christ himself, and that southwest France was the place to which the holy family fled after the crucifixion. A tad controversial, but it all adds to the atmosphere and mystery of this wonderful city, and it is a truly wonderful city. Despite the chronic traffic problem, it still retains the elegance and refinement of those glory years, now overlaid with the exuberance of its youthful population. It no longer enjoys the reputation for glamour and riches gained by its rivals Bordeaux and Nice and it doesn't share in the somewhat more dubious and raffish reputation of its Mediterranean neighbour, Marseille. Toulouse is hardworking, hot and definitely the place to be. If you take the energy of New York, the optimism and style of Sydney, the flavour of Florence and mix liberally with the distinctive architecture, history, wine and wonderful cuisine of the south of France, you have Toulouse.

It may not yet be the Paris of the south, but it will be.

★

After the splendour and colour of Toulouse, I decided that I really ought to become a little more acquainted with some of the other significant towns in the area.

Figeac is not an obvious point on the tourist trail. Tucked away in the Causses du Quercy at the tail end of the Massif Central and on the very northeastern outskirts of the Lot, it's a long way from the nearest motorway and you'd have to be really keen to see it. It isn't a very large town, and to be fair it's not particularly colourful, vibrant or even culturally significant. In fact as far as the visitor is concerned it's a bit of a backwater. However Figeac does have three weighty arguments in its favour. It's an old city on the banks of the lovely river Célé. It is without doubt beautiful, and it's had its moments of glory too. One of them came not so very long ago when a certain gentleman named Champollion, who owned a little bookshop in the town, produced a son who appeared to have a huge talent for linguistics. This precocious and well-read child grew up to be a bit of an academic and an expert in ancient languages. He was also obsessed with Egypt. In addition to the usual slugs, snails and puppy dogs tails that accumulate in the pockets of all schoolboys, he had rocks, relics, old bits of bone and Egyptian artefacts.

It wasn't until I rounded the corner of one of the ancient, winding alleyways in the town and found myself standing on a vast piece of polished marble covered in strange marks, that the significance of this hitherto unremembered gentleman suddenly struck me. Of course, Jean François Champollion! He translated the Rosetta Stone. One of the truly great achievements of archaeology, for by doing so he unlocked the long-hidden door to hieroglyphics and handed mankind the key to the ancient Egyptian world. Well!

I looked down, and I was actually standing on the stone itself! Scuttling hastily off, I looked round to see if anybody had seen me. Surely though, it wasn't possible for such a priceless archaeological treasure to be exposed to the ferocious elements of the Massif Central, not to mention any wandering female that might happen past. I noticed a large plaque on the wall and went to read it. I was quite right it wasn't possible; this was a splendid copy made for the bicentennial a couple of years before. The original was in the British Museum (naturally) along with the translation.

So the great M.Champollion was Figeac's most famous son. Now that I knew, he seemed to pop up all over the town and I wondered why I hadn't noticed the name before.* His father's *librarie* is now a museum in his honour, the tourist office is awash with him, the newer, less distinguished *libraries* defer to him and the central place has been renamed for him.

The ancient city is as old as most of the towns and cities round these parts, pre-Roman certainly, and substantially built of the grey stone of the hills on which it stands, designed to repel the Visigoths as well as the freezing winds and driving snow that characterise the Causses. The buildings are gloriously medieval, a few are older still, the streets and alleyways are as

* Since this was written the Champollion museum has been enlarged and moved to the Place Champollion in the centre of Figeac.

narrow as those of Cahors and Toulouse, but the city itself is quite different in both character and atmosphere. It somehow lacks the colour, vibrancy, the thronging street life and the ambiance of the previous two. It's a quieter, more introverted place, reminding me rather of the hilltop cities of Tuscany, and it probably hasn't changed very much in the past five hundred years. As I wandered down one of the narrowest streets, where the lumpy, uneven cobbles had probably never been replaced, I glanced up at the looming buildings, dark and haunting, the windows very high up. Halfway down, a drift of nuns passed silently through a two-metre thick gothic archway into an inner courtyard, heavily protected by an oak and iron gate.

At the end of the street one lone youth with black hair curling to his shoulders regarded me laconically. A few metres above his head there was a single, ancient stone balcony, the only one in the entire street. The strange feeling of otherworldliness was so insistent that I found myself looking round for a pomegranate tree.

★

The Causses boast several beautiful towns and countless beautiful villages. The crusaders were around here eight hundred years ago. Richard the Lionheart and his brother Henry were reputed to have got up to all sorts of slightly unchristian capers here. And one of the places that seems to come into many of the old tales is Rocamadour. It's not very far from Figeac, so that was my next port of call.

Rocamadour was originally just a small holy shrine dedicated to the Virgin. It's conveniently situated near one of the routes to Santiago de Compostella, so in view of its outstanding location and miraculous bell – which, legend has it, rings of its own accord when a miracle occurs – it's not surprising that it attracts a good many penitents.

One of the many treasures of this place is a statue; one of the famous 'Black Virgins' found in many places in southern France and Spain. (The Black Virgin is the patron saint of Catalonia) There's considerable controversy surrounding these statues and paintings. Some say they are merely another impression of the Madonna, others maintain that they are not images of the Madonna at all, but Mary Magdalene. We will probably never know. However of one fact we can be reasonably certain; in 1166 the body of an unknown hermit, who was said to have lived and died in a cave on the rock face itself, was discovered in a perfect state of preservation. This appeared to be yet another miracle and, in due course, the hermit was canonised St. Amadour. The town was named after him, more chapels were built, the great basilica was constructed and from that time on the shrine became a place of international pilgrimage and staggering wealth.

The site of this wonderful mini-city must be one of the most spectacular in France. It's built into, and out of, an almost sheer rock face rising from the Alzou valley. Heaven only knows how they managed to build it, but in view of its holy status perhaps that's the obvious answer. From the old town, halfway up the cliff face, you can still climb the great staircase – 216 rough-hewn steps – that the penitents used to ascend on their knees to the seven chapels above. There the relics of the saint lie in a holy haze of incense and absorb the murmur of prayer.

In days of old, when knights were a great deal bolder than was good for them, things got a little out of hand. Rocamadour, with all its treasures was laid waste several times in the wars of religion. It is said that Henry (known as the Young King because he was crowned during the lifetime of his father, Henry II) sacked Rocamadour to help pay his mercenaries. He died shortly afterwards at nearby Martel castle, reputedly struck down by the hand of God. Considering his mother, the illustrious Eleanor of Aquitaine, and his younger brother, Richard, were two of the most famous crusaders of the age, you'd have thought he'd have had just a little more consideration – or at least a little more sense.

I looked up at the awe-inspiring mass of pale ochre rock and tried to imagine what it must have been like when it was a real fortress. A few of the old gates remain but not much more. Thrusting my chilly hands deep in my pockets, I wandered off to see what the modern town was like.

Have you ever been to Cornwall? To the little places like Mousehole and Boscastle, which were once hauntingly beautiful little fishing villages, and are still beautiful except for the endless line of tourist traps. Postcards, ice cream, genuine bits of King Arthur's this, that or the other. Hotels, cream-teashops and souvenir shops selling every possible object you can think of made out of seashells. Rocamadour is a little like that. Not in the winter of course, because winter here is colder than the Arctic – it feels colder anyway – but in summer you can't move for tourists. Every single house in the town has been turned into a shop, a café or a hotel. A little train runs from the valley floor to the top of the city, bringing the tourists in their thousands, literally thousands, from the car parks below.

I bought a goat's cheese sandwich – a warm baguette longer than my forearm – from one of the dozen or so food stalls (Rocamadour is also famous for its *appellation controlée fromage de chevre,* made in the high farms around the city) and sat on a parapet looking up at the shrines. It really is an incredible sight; they seem to grow out of the cliff itself, wonderfully carved and crafted in glowing, golden rock. Stunningly beautiful, but sadly a little disfigured by the throngs.

But let's not lose our perspective here, Rocamadour is used to throngs, it was built for them, and in days gone by the many gates controlled them with apparent ease. But in days gone by the throngs were pilgrims; they didn't eat ice cream, they didn't scatter rubbish everywhere and they didn't pose for photographs every two minutes. There are still pilgrims, but every summer they are swamped by the tidal wave of *bronzée*, souvenir-hungry hoards. I suppose the people of the Causses are just trying to make a living, as we all are, and the tourists are only too happy to oblige them. One can't condemn it, but it's still sad.

From a distance you can't see any of this superficial scarring, and the view of the famous city is as breathtaking as ever. All the same, I thought wistfully, as I gazed across the wild hilltops where there's still no sign of any other village or even a dwelling, it's an ironic twist of fate that welcome tourists have done a far more thorough job of destroying this remote sanctuary than the vicious armies of Young Henry could possibly have managed.

★ ★ ★

Carrier Bag Pigeons And Wily Guinea Fowl

"Pigeons heading this way!" Our son and heir shouldered his way through the kitchen door, where we were enjoying a late supper and lingering over the cheese course. I peered out of the window expecting to see Francine's flock wheeling round the valley on their evening outing. There was nothing to see but a few late songbirds, hurrying home against the crimson backdrop of the setting Mediterranean sun, and a lone buzzard enjoying the thermals.

"Where?" I mumbled absentmindedly, more than half my attention given to a particularly squishy goat's cheese.

"There" he pointed in gleeful triumph, as the youngest inhabitant of the house came haring after him with a carrier bag stuffed with something distinctly feathery. Four pigeons, beautiful and obviously healthy, but indisputably dead. They were a gift from our generous neighbours. I'm not really squeamish, you can't be if you come to live in the heart of a country community, but I'm not awfully good at plucking and gutting pigeons, plucking anything in fact, and pigeons are particularly fiddly, although undeniably easier than plucking a goose! No, this is what our friend Rod terms, 'front of cave stuff' and the beloved rose to the challenge in true cavalier style. He decamped to the terrace, in weather cold enough to freeze your toes in seconds, and dealt swiftly and efficiently with both feathers and other less attractive detritus, presenting me with four splendid little birds – oven-ready – as we would have called them in our previous existence.

These I could deal with. "Pigeon pie or *pâté*?" I asked the gallant cavalier as he thawed his toes on Cruella. He didn't fancy either. What he'd really like, he told me, sitting back down to the abandoned cheese course, was *pigeons farcis*.

This is a stuffed pigeon dish that's eaten a fair bit round these parts. You can stuff them with anything you like of course. Sultanas and almonds – a popular one in our valley – a more hefty sausage meat and breadcrumbs, or any one of a dozen or more combinations of herbs, egg, vegetables or even couscous. We decided on the almond option, partly because we've got two almond trees in the garden, but mainly because we'd never had it before. It's a creation that has its roots firmly in North Africa, but so do many around these parts. France still has strong links with Morocco, a legacy of the French Protectorate of 1912. Besides, Morocco isn't all that far away, and the Moorish dishes that became so popular in Spain hundreds of years earlier, gradually percolated through the Pyrenees, first to Perpignan and then onwards and upwards as far north as the raw ingredients would grow. Round about here in fact.

"You'll have to bring some more wood up" I mused out loud, half my mind on pigeon stuffings, and half on the remains of the cheese platter. "It's going to be a red day tomorrow and I'll need a hot oven for the pigeons"

He looked up with a curious mixture of fright, delight and boys-own-adventure on his face.

"You sure?"

I nodded. "Yes, of course."

The reason for his curious reaction to my request, I must instantly explain, has nothing to do with pigeons. The EDF has an interesting system for charging electricity in the winter months. It's called the Tempo system, and only a Frenchman could have dreamed it up. You don't have to subscribe to this hair-brained scheme; if you're not disposed towards the speculative, you can pay a standard rate, but if you do decide to gamble you need to be on your toes or you can end up paying a great deal more than you bargained for.

It goes like this: Every day has a designated colour, red white or blue – naturally. An ordinary warm day is a blue day and costs three parts of bugger all. All summer days are blue days, which makes this system particularly attractive. A colder day is a white day and costs twice as much as a blue, but still not a great deal. A freezing cold day is a red day, costs ten times as much as a blue and substantially more than bugger all. The number of red days is finite, but there are still enough of them to give my dearly beloved heartburn. All the appliances are out of bounds; the cooker is certainly not tolerated – thank God for Cruella – and all the lights are switched off until accidents are imminent.

The meter – that lives downstairs in the cellars with the wine, a floating population of guinea pigs and the hibernating lemon trees – tells us what the next day's rate will be at 8 o 'clock each evening. A small messenger is sent to check just after the hour – except on Saturday, because Sundays and holidays are always blue days – and if the next day is to be a red day, the beloved will rush round the house disconnecting anything that might be switched on and accidentally burn money, most importantly of all, the washing machine and the loathed tumble-dryer.

Thus if I find, on the evening of a red day, that I have no clean knickers and the next day is also to be a red day, I am pretty well up the proverbial creek. Of course I can wash them by hand, but even if the next day is sunny, the temperatures will be below freezing, and as frozen drawers are not at all comfortable it means a kitchen festooned with underwear, which is neither beautiful nor desirable when a neighbour pops in for an aperitif. It's a complicated system, but it does give great scope for vast savings – or otherwise if you're not careful – and is therefore hugely popular with the rural French.

Early the next evening as I stoked Cruella and put the pigeons in to roast, I could hear the beloved singing to himself down in the cellars – and no doubt flicking switches and dancing round the junction box. All the mod-cons were turned off and there were game birds in the wood-fired oven. He was absolutely in his element.

⋆

A week after the pigeon episode I had another close encounter with an avian dinner menu.

The scene was an ancient stone-walled kitchen and I was jammed between the blackened beam of an old fireplace and a vast, prickly orange tree, brought in for the winter. I accepted a porcelain eggcup from my smiling hostess with every sign of rapturous pleasure and tentatively inspected the contents. The room certainly smelled of coffee but it also smelled strongly of soap and bleach and I felt it prudent to check. Having ascertained that the steaming little handful of white porcelain did indeed contain liquid refreshment, I glanced furtively at my neighbours and knocked it back in one.

"Jesus, Mary and Joseph!" – As an Irish friend of mine put it, when first introduced to a similar brew – "It's as dense, dark and strong as the peat bogs of old Ireland." The simile had substance; ten minutes later I was still surreptitiously chewing.

Parties are thin on the ground in the post festive-season weeks – mind you, houses are also a bit thin on the ground round these parts – so when my friend invited me to this one I felt somewhat obliged to attend. Besides, I was ready for some company. A famous misconception in this land of gastronomy is that all parties are glamorous, Champagne soaked, *foie gras* stuffed affairs. They certainly aren't. This one wouldn't be black tie/posh frock, it wouldn't even be smart/casual, in fact overalls would have been more appropriate. It was, Marie-Blanche intoned, throwing her arms about in a fair imitation of Julie Andrews on a mountaintop, a clean, fresh sort of party. I was mightily intrigued; what exactly did she mean by that? She shrugged as my wavering French and her non-existent English failed us, but by this time she'd already decided, I was definitely going.

Two days later I followed my leader cautiously along the narrow, twisting road that winds up from the mist-shrouded Lot valley. There were no other cars, but there's always the risk of landing a fleeing deer on the bonnet, not to mention *sanglier*. Marie-Blanche obviously had no such fears, or maybe the car was in such an advanced state of dilapidation it wouldn't have made a great deal of difference anyway, but for whatever reason, after five short minutes she was completely out of sight. I muttered blasphemous expletives to myself. Now I'd have to find this house *tout seul*, and in the mist! She might have waited for me. I wallowed in self-pity and swerved crossly round a particularly sharp hairpin, narrowly missing a tractor and rusty trailer piled high with muck. The hoary driver, beret protecting his head, scarf tucked well into his padded dungarees, looked regretfully at the precious pile he'd just deposited behind him, then regarded me with a lugubrious countenance. I smiled apologetically and manoeuvred myself back onto the narrow track that served as a road. The mist began to clear at that point, and as I climbed steadily upwards I finally burst out into brilliant sunshine. Spirits lifting, I made greater use of the accelerator, but it was still another ten minutes before I stumbled on the venue for the afternoon's entertainment. Turning onto an unmade *chemin rural* with a terraced vineyard on one side and the ubiquitous oak woods on the other, I spied a sprawling cluster of ancient stones. No name or sign of course, but the half dozen cars in the uneven gravelled space under the walnut tree made it a pretty sure bet.

My hostess threw open the door.

"Amarndar!" She shrieked delightedly, which is about as close as they can get to my given name in the southwestern accent. She removed the black cheroot she seems to use in place of chewing gum and gave me a customary embrace. I was hauled in, introduced and subjected to thirty more kisses as the fifteen ladies present eyed me with childlike interest. An exotic species, English, and game to mix with the natives.

Marie-Blanche took my coat and added it to a pile somewhere in the depths of the old stone farmhouse, apologising profusely all the while for not realising that I wasn't right on her bumper. My hostess threw open the thick oak door to the delicious warmth of her ancient kitchen and the mystery was revealed.

Laid out on the long, scrubbed farmhouse table was a vast selection of all the cleaning products the good French housewife could possibly need for a clean, fresh abode. Unfortunately though, I'm not a good French housewife; I'm not even a good English housewife. Cleaning is anathema to me, as my dear family will happily testify. This would be a trial undertaken with all the grit of an ancient Christian martyr, you could almost smell the burning – or maybe that was the coffee – in the name of good relations.

It was about this point in the proceedings that the eggcups were produced and my taste buds effectively numbed for the rest of the day, but on with the real business.

A lavishly endowed lady, with a taste for French-Navy, began to talk us through the miraculous products on offer. The ridiculous notion of using bleach – *nom de dieu!* – when you had a septic tank, as we all have in the little hamlets and scattered farms, is a quite barbarous notion. The audience nodded vigorously, clutching their eggcups. Maelle, our hostess, circulated with more steaming black coffee, I was still chewing the last lot, but held out my eggcup obediently and wondered if I could possibly press the orange tree into service. Then at a given signal, and with some ceremony, chairs were scraped back, Madame French-Navy puffed herself up like a portly adder and we were shocked into placing our orders. The prices were scandalously high. I suppose it works like an old-fashioned Tupperware party, the sort of thing my mother used to attend in the seventies. But I didn't need any of that stuff. Ladies were actually discussing the varying merits of rival floor cloths…

Had my social-life honestly deteriorated that much?

Fortunately for my sanity and my chequebook, a diversion was caused at that point. The two young children of the house careered through the kitchen in pursuit of a large guinea fowl. As this was Saturday afternoon, the bird in question may well have been destined to be the leading light at Sunday lunch and was understandably reluctant to perform. As it was mid-January and colder than the frozen wastes of Siberia, all doors and windows were tightly closed. With no way out, the hapless fowl raced round the kitchen like an avian greyhound with the two children in full cry on his tail. As the bird shot between Madame French-Navy's stout ankles, child number one grabbed the poor lady's knee to get a better angle on the chase and over she went, cannoning into several other startled ladies – all clutching remains of the peat bogs of old Ireland – and ending up spread-eagled on the ancient stone flags of the kitchen floor. Pandemonium ensued. The children screamed at the bird, the bird flapped wildly in panic, upsetting the coffee pot on the edge of the table, which crashed to the floor scattering glass and liquid far and wide, whilst the poor lady gasped and wallowed like a landed tuna.

We hauled her to her feet, hurriedly straightening her garments to hide an arresting expanse of salmon-pink frill, and deposited her gently in a large *fauteuil*. Louise fanned her gently and sponged the stains off her remarkably accommodating dress. Marie-Blanche put one of the floor cloths to excellent use, eradicating the mini-bogs that had formed, whilst others employed the dustpan and brush with ferocious efficiency. Meanwhile Maelle ushered the children out of the room and reprieved the Sunday lunch menu by opening the doors to the terrace.

"Merci, oh merci bien... desolé," muttered the victim of the fray in exhausted accents, *"trés desolé!"*

She needn't have been. I can't speak for my companions of course, but personally I was exceedingly grateful to her, partly for bringing the sales pitch to an effective close and partly for dispensing with the means of delivering any further liquid refreshment.

Maelle returned from liberating the cause of the fracas, to offer Madame French-Navy something to revive her; eau-de vie – literally water of life – rather appropriate as she certainly looked in need of reviving. However, if you've never tried it, take my word for it. It's strong stuff. This particular potion was an eau-de-vie *pruneaux maison*. The pride and joy of Maelle's father and powerful enough to lay you out after one glass. Madame knocked it back with lip-smacking relish and began to make an astonishingly swift recovery. She requested a refill, which was immediately forthcoming, and just as quickly dispatched. Several other ladies, sparked into action, began to attack the contents of a large dark *armoire* in the corner. Apéritifs were laid out, a large terrine emerged from the cellars beneath the house and several baguettes were systematically sawn up at the other end of the long kitchen table. This was going on for some time yet.

I decided it might just be an appropriate moment to make my bow. So, improvising at a feverish rate, I wimpily excused myself from the apéritifs and possible dinner to follow and escaped into the cold, sunny air of the farmyard.

In the corner, by a decaying stone barn, the star of the show eyed me truculently. I nodded at him in a half-salute. I was indeed grateful that he'd brought the proceedings to an effective halt, but all the same I hadn't previously realised just how much fun my friends had at these affairs. Next time I would be more prepared. The parties in this rural backwater of southern France may not always be glamorous, but they're certainly a breath of fresh air.

★ ★ ★

Villages Ending In Ac

As the world emerged from the excesses of the festive season, the little villages of the Quercy were preparing for the advent of spring. Late pruning must be attended to, spraying and replanting must be done quickly before the sap began to rise.

There appeared to be high jinks going on in the vineyard below us. Several lines of newly planted vines were being covered with straw, presumably to protect them from the vicious late frosts, and four large bales stood at the head of the lines ready to be broken up and spread as required. It was lunch time and the workers were leaning comfortably against the tractor, enjoying the sunshine, taking liberal swigs of wine and huge bites out of baguettes stuffed with *rillettes* or *saussison sèche*. Laughter echoed round the valley, blue rinsed chins wobbled and Gauloises wagged, until a sudden shout alerted the merry band to the extraordinary fact that one of the bales appeared to be on the move, more than that, it seemed to be on fire. Under my startled gaze the rogue bale bounced happily down the vineyard, leaving a blazing trail of charred grasses and vine clippings in its wake. Twenty metres behind it, half a dozen arm-waving vignerons chased madly, bottle in one hand and cigarette in the other. Having caught up with their mobile bonfire they hopped around it, obviously a little unsure of their ground. A few tried poking with a stick, one tried to kick it into submission – which didn't seem terribly prudent. In the end it collapsed to a flaming heap and they left it to burn itself out.

As the afternoon wore on the pace of the workers slackened perceptibly, it's tiring work pruning vines, although maybe in this case it had something to do with the lunchtime tipple. I glimpsed them from time to time as I worked in the garden; they were bent almost double with their backs to the wind, four blue bums in a row.

By early evening, as the late winter sun was beginning to set behind the hills, the workers packed up their tools and eased their aching limbs. The vines were immaculate. The majority neatly pruned, with three rows tucked up under a golden blanket beside a mischievous-looking long, black snake, still gently steaming in the twilight. Perhaps no smoking in the vineyards would be an advisable rule I thought to myself as I watched the procession of curiously narrow little tractors coughing and spluttering and finally emerging from the safety of the vines to set off in a line towards the little hamlet of Cenac.

Cenac is one of those places that looks just the same now as it always has. A stone church, a few stone houses clustered around it and a memorial to their brave sons. The narrow road is frequently sprinkled with straw and muck or squashed grapes – depending on the season – and too rough and winding for any sort of speed. From a distance you can see that it sits on the crest of a hill. In fact it's the village that holds centre stage in the view from our western terrace. Vineyards, walnut groves and oak woods slip gently away from it and every now and then a farmhouse or battered old barn will punctuate the landscape, just to add a little authenticity. It is quietly beautiful and because it's as far from the beaten track as it's possible to go without abandoning your car, it will stay that way. There are hundreds of villages and hamlets like it in this little corner of France. Most were built with one eye to defence and so either sit on the crest of a hill, or sport impressive bastide walls, sometimes both. Another peculiarity that characterises this area, and one that I adore, is the suffix *'ac'*. Almost every other village and town proclaims its location in its name. Within our immediate locality we have not only Cenac, but also Prayssac, Cayrac, Rouffiac, Cambayrac, Crayssac, Carnac and umpteen others. It's supposedly a hangover from the Romans – naturally – and is said to be derived from the Latin *'iacia'*, meaning to own. Thus our own little hamlet of Cenac would perhaps have belonged to a man called Cen. The practice spreads at least as far north as Limoges and as far south as Toulouse; just one more of the quintessential quirks of the Quercy.

*

"Come and have a look at this!"

My son led me across the gravel drive and over to the rocky bank between the swimming pool and the pine copse. He stopped me twenty metres short and pointed.

"What's that?" I squinted in the general direction of his dancing finger. It looked like a long, thin skipping rope laid out over the rocks, or perhaps a very skinny snake. "Well?" he prompted, hopping from foot to foot.

"I don't know, it's not… it's not a snake is it?"

"No!" He could hardly contain himself, and half dragged me to the site of the phenomenon.

"Good heavens!" I bent down to examine the rope. It was certainly living, but it wasn't a snake, it was a long, long line of hairy caterpillars, each one attached to the one in front, nose to tail. They were moving purposefully – at caterpillar pace of course – to where the lavender bushes billowed over the far side of the gravel drive like ladies' crinolines. A sort of furry follow-my-leader, I'd never seen anything like it. Each specimen was about three or four centimetres long and there were a hundred and eighteen of them. How very peculiar.

An hour or so later as we gathered for lunch, I recounted the tale to the beloved. He was mightily impressed with the marvel, but tempered our enthusiasm with a timely warning.

"One hundred and eighteen caterpillars," he pointed out dampeningly, "could cause a fair bit of damage to one of your new trees."

I stopped mid-chew. He was right, and they were heading straight for the young olives. We scraped back chairs and rushed out to the scene of the crime. They hadn't got very far; thankfully gravel is not ideal territory for a hairy caterpillar.

"Head them off at the pass!" Suggested my son, waving the end of his baguette at the caterpillar-in-command. "Call out the cavalry, load the cannons!"

The beloved, meanwhile, was thoughtfully recording their presence with the digital camera.

"We need to find out what they are." He said, decisively.

"Caterpillars!" My son was in party mood by this time, and was banished back to the dining table to finish his lunch while we mulled over the problem in a thoughtful silence. I'd already attempted identification with the help of a butterfly and moth tome. But no dice, there were hundreds of caterpillars that looked just like these.

"Internet!" Exclaimed the beloved, having a eureka moment whilst finishing his wildlife photography, and be quick!"

The task had obviously been delegated to me, so I mooched into the study to begin investigations. After all, I mused, there can't be many caterpillars that behave like this, and I was right, there aren't. In fact there's only one; the Pine Processionary Moth caterpillar. It's an unmitigated pest in the Mediterranean and causes widespread damage to pine forests. Which would explain why two of our trees were looking a little jaundiced. It builds itself a cocoon in the tall pines; you can see them hanging like large tangles of Angel Hair on Christmas trees. Apparently all the caterpillars troop down in mid-winter – nose to tail – looking for some soft ground to burrow and pupate. They also move from tree to tree in the same manner, very strange. But even more alarming, they're poisonous.

"The poison," I read, "is contained in the hairs; the caterpillars should not, therefore, be handled." Oh dear. It went on to inform me that even after death the caterpillar can shed these poisonous shafts, causing rashes and intense irritation. Oh dear, oh dear. I went out to report the findings to the naturalist in charge. He nodded imperturbably, and asked for the old fish tank.

"Pardon?" I asked, wondering if I'd heard him right.

"Send one of the children for the little fish tank. It's down on the lower terrace – and find me some chopsticks."

It's usually best not to argue when the beloved has set himself on some irrevocable course. This was obviously one of those times. I sent my son for the required tank and trundled off to retrieve the Chinese cutlery.

When I got back to the scene of the action, the operation was in full swing. The beloved had fashioned himself makeshift chopsticks out of old twigs and was picking up the caterpillars one by one and loading them into the tank. My son, meanwhile, had found a breakaway train, bringing the total number of villains to two hundred. All were picked up and temporarily relocated.

"There!"The beloved exhaled in satisfaction. He put the lid on the tank and pulled the car keys out of his pocket. "Now go and sit in the front."

"Me?" I asked warily.

"Yes, of course, come on, quickly!" He opened the door for me, and placed the tank gently on my knees, where I eyed the inhabitants with doubtful enthusiasm.

"We'll take them to that pine wood outside Carnac," he thrust the car into reverse, "and tip them out on the soft bit, where they were moving the vines."

"Wagons Ho!"Yelled my son, irrepressibly.

Two hundred Pine Processionary Moth Caterpillars, sorted.

★

That winter the beloved had finally come to a painful decision; despite the low tide in our coffers, we needed to do something about rebuilding some of the essential elements of our garden, and a fairly large quantity of stone would be needed to achieve the desired result. There was a fair old bit just lying around our land, in the woods and at the edge of the paths, not to mention our ancient and collapsed terraces. But the terraces would eventually need to be restored and the smaller rocks that were scattered so liberally were just a bit too small for some of the more urgent tasks. The virtually non-existent front doorstep was the first task in the queue and for that we needed something bigger, and preferably flatter. Crayssac, we were assured, would be the place to find it. So one sunny Monday afternoon we set out to find our stone.

The village of Crayssac is in two parts. One part contains the traditional huddle of stone houses, church and tiny school, and unlike most villages in these parts, the stone is particularly neat and well pointed; the other part is just a straggle along the fast D811. But it's a straggle entirely devoted to stone in all its forms. There are quarries and stone-cutting yards, garden furniture, paving and even statuary. There's gravel and shingle and vast blocks of uncut Quercy stone. There was such an embarrassment of choice that we pulled over onto a dusty verge to discuss which yard was which, because it wasn't at all clear.

"I think," the beloved announced after ten minutes of irresolute dithering, "we should go and ask one of those men."

The persons in question, a shady looking bunch, dressed in faded *bleu* and surrounded by a colour co-ordinated plume of smoke and dust, turned out to be a gang of seasonal labourers, taking their ease after a hard morning's work at the quarry. They suggested the yard on the corner as our best bet for large, flat pieces of durable stone and pointed the way to the *bureau*. I peered out of the car window to where they were waving. It was a minute building, about the size of a small garden shed, built precisely with beautifully cut stone and so liberally dusted with mason's icing sugar that it looked almost as if it were made of concrete, which in my private opinion rather defeated the object of building with stone in the first place.

To say that we got a little carried away barely hints at the scale of the thing. There was stone of every size, every colour, and every thickness. Carved stone, dressed stone, rough stone, white stone and even marble. We were dazzled and more than a little puzzled. Where on earth should one start? Naturally, the man-in-charge ignored us for a good twenty minutes, politely giving us time to wander round and make several large, hasty and unwise decisions. We chose a nice rough, flattish stone for the doorstep – might as well re-do the *bolet* at the same time – we decided we'd have ten square metres. And what about the wall we needed to construct round the swimming pool? A rustic local white would be the thing, not too rough of course; after all we'd have to build it ourselves. We found the perfect candidate. The beloved looked at me thoughtfully, as if guessing the weight of a prize sow.

"I think we'll need about four cubic metres." He announced, as if he'd just loaded up a supermarket trolley with four boxes of cornflakes. "We'll have to have it delivered of course." Not only would we need the stone delivered, I thought, beginning to wonder if this was such a brilliant idea, but a workforce too. Four cubic metres of stone would need the equivalent of four hundred Egyptian slaves to move it.

"What about the rock at the entrance to the drive, for the house name?" he continued, getting into his stride – there are some big stones over there."

There were indeed; they were about the size of a small sofa. I ventured hesitantly that they might be just a little larger than necessary. Even half that size would be impossible to move. He eyed the massive forms regretfully. "Hmmm, you might be right, I'll ask him if he's got anything smaller."

By this time a wiry man in collar to toe, once *bleu* now very *gris* overalls, comprehensively dusted with chalk, had joined us and was adding his own unique slant to the buy-one-get-one-free approach to sales. The beloved acquainted him with the result of the morning's deliberations and asked about the smaller piece for the entrance.

"Pas de problème," he had the very thing, over there, in the corner, behind the forklift. I was a little apprehensive. The massive forms he indicated were certainly smaller than the original blocks, which were presumably waiting until somebody needed stone to re-build one of the great pyramids, but they were hardly – well – domestic size.

"Parfait!" enthused the beloved, "we'll have that one."

"A plaisir Monsieur, gratuit." He was so encouraged with the vast shopping list we'd already identified that he was throwing – well, heaving – in the vast block for nothing! The beloved was flushed, transcendent with heady triumph. Probably glad to see the back of it, I muttered sourly. This whole expedition was

getting a little out of hand. The small wiry man – who revelled in the name of Eusebio Pinto – began to get down to business. Which of the several sorts of rough building stone did we require? Ah.

"This one is of course the very best," he said, indicating a very smooth variety, cut on three sides, "for skilled masons really". He proudly pointed out the cornerstones and took us on a rapid tour of the exquisite features one could construct with such perfectly cut stone. The next was a little rougher and "perfect for garden walls," our mentor informed us, "those over there"; he indicated our original choice, *"pouf! Trés rustique."* He mentioned a startlingly low price and the beloved's eyes lit up like a child's on Christmas morning.

"Yep, that's the one, I think we might as well have five," he informed Eusebio.

I put my head in my hands.

*

The nearest town to our little piece of hillside is Prayssac. It's also the setting for the best Friday market around. The locals like Friday markets; they can do all their shopping for the weekend in one go. Vegetables and fish are bought at a leisurely pace from immaculately laid out market stalls. No portion, however large or small is too much trouble. Bread comes from one of the favoured *boulangeries*, meat from the outstanding *boucherie*, if they can afford it, eggs or a live rabbit from the man-with-a-van if they can't. A viola or two to replace the one the cat knocked off the windowsill, or a geranium in summer. The other odds and ends can be found at the supermarket when all the important transactions have been made. Friday morning in Prayssac is a scrum.

I walked down the Rue Aristide Briand, past the café/bar

at the end and along the edge of the *pétanque* court to the church that stood serenely in the middle of the hubbub. The-man-with-a-van caught my eye as I made my way over the cobbled square. I was late that morning and he hadn't got many eggs left. I always buy from him, partly because his eggs are always fresh and therefore always sell out by ten-thirty, partly because they're very reasonably priced and partly because he's local and always there. The one thing I find a bit of a hurdle is his pricing strategy. I like my eggs large and naturally I expect to pay more for them, but not here. All the eggs are the same price, if you want to pick out your own – and most people do – he gives you a box and leaves you to it. (If you're organised you bring your own box, but I'm afraid I'm not very, and I rarely remember) He sells them all anyway, he told me once, so what's the point in pricing his eggs separately? That day he'd put a box by for me, he often does this and it's so very kind of him that I often feel guilty. I don't always make it to this market, but every time this sort of thing happens I realise that I must, simply must, make more effort. I'm an intrinsic part of this community now and if they expect me I shouldn't let them down.

The first time I was presented with my specially saved box I thought it must be just one of many he put by for any latecomer he recognised, but it's not so. One of my fellow marketeers, a little grey-haired lady with matching dog, likes her eggs small, very small. I noticed as she was picking them out, that she prefers the white ones. She buys a dozen at a time and he will hand her an extra one – which goes precariously into her coat pocket – as a bonus. She too has her boxes put by if she happens to be late, but her choice is very different from mine.

I handed over my euro, admired his new umbrella and moved on to the small vegetable stall opposite. This is another one-man-band affair and the produce changes almost weekly.

On this particular day it was still too early for spring vegetables and greenery was in short supply. He was displaying the last of the winter cabbages, piles of the ubiquitous leeks, vast clumps of Swiss chard and a heap of juicy, bitter endives. He also had a box of muddy looking tubers that I suspected may turn out to be Jerusalem artichokes.

"Bien sûr, Madame!" Of course they were, how could I possibly doubt it? Because they were completely camouflaged with mud I thought to myself. He generously brushed away the worst of it before weighing them, and threw in an extra couple anyway. I bought four large leeks, fat, damp and still rooted, and a large slice of golden pumpkin.

"Persil?" He asked. I nodded and thanked him. All the vegetable stallholders have a box of parsley at the back, and if you make a large purchase, or if you're a regular, they'll throw in a handful. That same handful would cost you about a euro if you bought it. It's a common and generous gesture.

In the queue outside the cheese van, I eyed the sumptuous looking Bleu des Causses, my current favourite; they'd got plenty of little *cabecous* too. The only other item I needed that morning was a warm, golden *poulet rôti* from the man by the statue of Madonna and Child. He sells his own free-range chickens, beautifully basted, and lip-smackingly succulent. Just the aroma of roast chicken, on that chilly winter day, was heavenly. I wandered down past the church to the café Tisany, succumbing rather guiltily to a splendid wheel of sticky *tarte aux noix* on the way. Slumping in a chair in the steamy interior I ordered a *grand créme*, and whilst waiting for the waitress to deal with my order I took a quick peep inside my egg box. They were all enormous.

* * *

A Dish Fit For The Gods

The southern regions of France have produced a great many rich and glorious dishes that are imitated the world over. They also have a great many distinctive foods. The vast trawl from the aquamarine waters of the Mediterranean springs naturally to mind; the glorious, garlicky Bouillabaisse taking pride of place on the coast, with the olives and numerous herbs of Provence providing salads that sigh warm weather.

Further west there's the truffle, *foie gras* – naturally – and every other part of the numerous geese and ducks. There are also the outstanding, colourful and marvellously diverse vegetables. Everybody nowadays eats courgettes and peppers, aubergines, artichokes and huge tomatoes, peaches, melons and cherries. But what about the most famous of them all, the haricot bean?

French markets are piled high – literally piled – with vast amounts of *haricots verts* in the summer months, and as the white heat of August slides almost imperceptibly into an extended, balmy autumn, sacks of the drying *haricots blancs*, still in their pods, are sold in huge numbers. French beans are grown and sold all over the world, but rarely in such copious amounts for the ordinary man in the street to buy, and sadly not always available in markets. So what does the French housewife do with them all?

Well, *haricots verts* are an easy option, they are a marvellous green vegetable, you can add them to salads, stir-fry them – not that a rural French woman would ever dream of doing so – and use them to accompany just about anything but the breakfast croissants. But what about the *haricots blancs?* The plump fully-grown beans, either fresh or dried.

They form the base of what may arguably be described as the most famous dish of them all. A dish that combines the nutritious beans with the beloved goose or duck and the equally revered Toulouse sausage. If you live in Carcassonne you might conceivably add a little lamb and possibly a game bird. If you live in Castelnaudry (where they claim fiercely that their recipe is the original) you would certainly add pork and bacon. But in Toulouse and in most parts of the Quercy most recipes use just the *confits d'oie* (or *canard*) perhaps a hunk of *poitrine*, a good metre or so of the splendid sausage and the freshest, plumpest *haricots*.

It is, of course, the magnificent cassoulet. A truly ancient dish that has been prepared in this part of France for hundreds of years. Its origins are decidedly murky, it supposedly emerged during the hundred years war and possibly much earlier, but there's a great deal of heated ongoing debate over the issue. In the end I suspect that, like most of the other great casserole dishes of Europe, it's merely a dish based on local produce – in this case the outstanding beans of the area and whatever else that could be grown or caught – that gradually evolved over the years.

It's appropriate really that such a marvellous *pièce de résistance* should be irrevocably linked to a fabulous city like Toulouse, because there is no feast more fit for the Gods. And let's face it; if the numerous grail legends happen to be right and there really are descendants of Christ, and they really did settle in Aquitaine, (two rather large assumptions, I grant you) then undoubtedly they would be feasting upon this dish.

*

It was one bitterly cold morning in the final throws of winter that I decided to subject my eight dinner guests that evening to a gastronomic orgy. If you're going to serve a cassoulet, it's really only fair to warn guests in advance, as this is possibly the most filling dish in the world. It's prudent not to eat for several hours before it and impossible to eat for several hours afterwards. I reached for the phone and did my duty.

The thought of this treat in store was greeted with universal delight, which rather put me on my mettle. On a freezing night, when the wind batters the shutters and the mercury is as low as you've seen it, there's nothing like a huge, steaming cassoulet to warm the heart – and various other more peripheral bits of the body – and lift the flagging spirits. I flexed my fingers, sharpened my kitchen knives and sallied forth to reconnoitre the wealth of available ingredients.

Cahors market was half deserted that morning, the tops of the canopies hoary with a late frost. Muffled stallholders were warming their hands on plastic cups of coffee or warming their stomachs with swigs of red wine, stamping their booted feet to keep the circulation from giving up entirely. The butcher's breath reached me like wisps of cloud as I bent over the tangled metres of sausage.

"Avec ça Madame?" He asked, as I decided about a metre or so would amply feed the ten of us.

"Les cuisses de canard confits, s'il vous plait," I murmured, and watched interestedly as my words floated across the glass counter in a frozen cloud. He began throwing the confits around with practised fingers the size and shape of his own sausages, showing me each one and waiting for a verdict before adding it to the growing pile on the paper. I selected ten prize specimens. A small piece of belly pork – *poitrine* – completed the meat purchases.

I like to use this stall. The butcher is actually a *fermier* from the slightly flatter plains around Lalbenque. He raises geese, ducks, chickens and pigs in open fields and, naturally, he makes his own sausage and *pâtés*.

He grinned and joked, "Hope you've got somebody to share this with!"

I smiled weakly and stamped my feet, my nose was beginning to freeze over. Handing over the required euros and accepting a free slice of *pâté maison* with as much grace as I could muster, I thanked him and scuttled quickly over to the fruit and vegetable stalls where at least it was self-service and I could get a move on. Six vast tomatoes, a bunch of carrots – straight from the soil – a kilo of onions and a fistful of fresh parsley, perhaps a leek or two for flavour, and I could be on my way.

"We have some fresh cardoons in this morning, Madame", the young lad on the stall encouraged me, brandishing an enormous example and almost relieving me of my scarf. "Very delicious, very tender!"

I hesitated; I didn't really have any use for cardoons that day.

"You can try some free, yes?" He poked a few sticks in my

carrier bag. My eyes watered as I tried to thank him. My nose had given up the struggle and was now completely dormant. I took my bag, fumbled the change in frozen hands, and scurried thankfully across the market square and down the Rue Georges Clemenceau to the steamy warmth of the café.

The waiter, short-sleeved and lively as ever, eyed me with an amused grin, he didn't say anything, merely brought me an enormous cup of steaming *café crème*, placed the bill under the ashtray then picked up my hands and placed them round the cup.

"Voila Madame!"

I'm never quite sure whether he's flirting with me or whether this is the way he treats every regular customer. Either way I was quite grateful when he was called away; my frozen extremities were beginning to thaw at an alarmingly embarrassing rate. I cradled the cup blissfully, took a few sips of hot, foamy deliciousness and thawed like an ice cube in a sauna. Burrowing in my bag for an ancient tissue that I was sure was in there somewhere, I came across the cassoulet shopping list.

I blew my nose as discreetly as possible, wiped my eyes and made a mental note to pop in to the *boulangerie* for some suitable bread. I also had to call in on my old friend M. Dompierre to pick up a couple of kilos of last summer's beans, to replace the ones I'd put in soak that morning and I reminded myself, I really must remember to stop at the Château Couillac on the way back to pick up five litres of last year's vintage. Then, with such outstanding ingredients at my disposal, all I had to do was construct the masterpiece.

You have to be careful if you're intending to serve cassoulet in southwest France. Every town's defined recipe differs from every other town's defined recipe, there are also master cooks who know more about the subject than you ever could, and old family recipes to throw into the melting pot as well. Fortunately my guests that night were unlikely to be too critical. Four of them were English – so no problem there – and of the four French guests, two were immigrants to the area, having fled from the non-stop grind of Paris to the slow and carefree delights of this lovely place, and two were in their twenties, much too young to be overly bossy about food.

My waiter was back with the lunch menu.

"I'm sorry, I really can't today," I told him, "I've got a dinner party tonight, and it's cassoulet."

"Ah," he nodded understandingly, "then you will be needing only a very little Madame, to keep up your strength. We have oysters today. Six or twelve?"

"No, really Florian, I don't have time, I've still got loads to do."

He looked at me gravely,

"Have you put the beans to soak?"

"Oh well, yes, of course," I said indignantly, thanking my stars that I'd at least thought of that.

"Then there is not a very great hurry, and you will enjoy very much some oysters don't you think?" He gave me a little nudge that almost knocked me into my *café crème*.

"But I've got to get the wine yet, and … oh, *d'accord* Florian, I'd love some oysters."

It was half past two by the time I finally escaped his clutches, and apart from being waylaid by oysters I'd also been cajoled into a tipple at the Château Couillac. I was desperately late by the time I pulled into my own little drive.

Back in the warm, steamy kitchen, I stoked Cruella and fed another log into her yawning red mouth, shed my coat and turned on the beans; about one and a half kilos and a good sprinkling of coarse sea salt from the vast flats of the Camargue. Whilst they were coming to the boil, I laid out the results of my morning's haul. I love the look of a long Toulouse sausage, you can't buy them like this in England – well not very easily – and it was a novel feeling to grab one end of it and be mindful of the fact that if I accidentally nudged it off the table, the other end would sweep the floor.The *confits* were delightful too; moist, plump joints of duck, swathed in their own delectable, and warmly calorific, fat.The piece of pork rind was a thick, slightly bristly hunk of flavouring with a fair bit of meat still on it. Beats gravy granules! I thought wryly to myself as I thumped it on the table with the rest of the meat.

One of the wonderful things about a cassoulet is that you can put the whole lot into one pot and just leave it to fend for itself for the majority of the time whilst you get on with the million and one other things on your list.

A mournful whimper from the back door reminded me of one of the things on my list. I fumbled with the key and yanked open the stiffly frozen door, only to be met by a very reproachful Labrador.

'You forgot my breakfast treat, what have you got to say for yourself?'The accusation was evident in every indignant line of her significantly over-padded body.

"Sorry Tinia" I mumbled, daft as a cuckoo clock, and broke a sizable length from the fresh baguette for her. Her tail swept the terrace as she automatically sat, total forgiveness replacing indignation. She accepted the peace offering – her favourite – and took it out to one of the scrubby patches of land that we refer to as lawns. Lying down, she carefully held it between massive golden paws and enjoyably gnawed it like a bone until there was nothing left but a crumb.

Meanwhile, I was starting to assemble the highlight of the evening. Onion, garlic, pork and a sprig of bay all simmered gently in a little duck fat, then the sausages, which, for ease at the table, were cut into portions.

I once shared a cassoulet with about twenty others, and the

cook had left the sausage whole. It was New Years Eve, everybody was in high spirits – in every sense of the word – and it seemed a great lark when the two or three metres of sausage slithered all over the table like an out of control Boa Constrictor. But as a general rule, and in the interests of hygiene, I prefer to cut it up.

Next into the pot were the splendid *confits*. I like to use duck for my cassoulets. Goose is wonderful, but a *cuisse d'oie* is huge, and with the best will in the world you cannot get it into a person-sized portion, not if you're going to accompany it with pork, sausage and beans anyway.

I carried the beans to the sink and drained them, rinsing them thoroughly. Elizabeth David – that doyenne of the Mediterranean kitchen – maintained that the women of the Languedoc would never tip their bean water down the sink because it would make it stink for a full 24 hours. What's more she suggested they would bottle it and use it as a cleaning fluid, which rather makes me wonder what the hell must be in an uncooked, dried bean. However my bean water does go down the sink, maybe the septic tanks are a little more sophisticated nowadays, or perhaps I'm just not as fussy, but I've never actually noticed a stink.

I turned my attention back to the pot, and you need a big one for an authentic cassoulet. For a start, it really isn't the sort of dish you can serve for two or three people, it's a family Sunday lunch favourite or a proper feast dish, rarely made for less than six and often for over a hundred at numerous village fêtes all over the south. My pot is a capacious, glazed earthenware affair that only just fits in Cruella's rather slender oven (that of course is where the name comes from, the *cassole* is the original earthenware open casserole), and once full is too heavy to be moved far without the aid of a little finely honed muscle.

The general rule with this dish is to fry anything that needs frying in advance. Boil the beans for at least an hour and a half (unless you're using this year's beans, still in the pods, in which case you just bring them to the boil, throw away the first lot of water – because Elizabeth knows best – and add your herbs and tomatoes, before bringing them to the boil again), then layer all the ingredients in the pot. Finally, add the broth from the beans ready for the final baking, which can take anything up to another three hours, depending on which recipe you choose to follow.

Along with most authorities on the subject, I add a good sprinkling of breadcrumbs to my cassoulet just before I slide it into the oven. This forms a crust, which helps to prevent evaporation. It can be broken in places from time to time, and more broth added where you break it.

I layered my beans with slices of tomato from nearby Marmande, bay leaves from the trees by the front door and thyme from the hillsides. Of course there were the two red onions and ten cloves of garlic I had fried earlier to be added in artistically spaced spoonfuls, then in went the lightly fried sausage, neatly cut into twelve pieces, just in case somebody wanted seconds – I've never known it happen but there's always a first time – more beans and tomatoes, more onion and garlic, then the *confits*. I like to arrange them so that the ends stick out of the finished ensemble, it looks more interesting and it makes it easier to serve in equal portions, especially if you're catering for a crowd, and one generally is when serving cassoulet. Finally I added the last of the beans and very carefully seasoned the broth – one doesn't get a second chance. I sprinkled the breadcrumbs and lightly drizzled the whole with olive oil. It was at this point that my own talents ground to a halt and I had to hunt down some working muscle.

The beloved emerged from his study looking like

Rumplestiltskin's older brother, but his was the only muscle available, so he had to do the business. Together we heaved and squeezed the vast concoction into Cruella's gaping oven, where, for two and a half hours, the flavours would gently mingle and the beans bake to a luscious, creamy consistency. The savoury scent issuing from the kitchen made my tummy twist with longing. I had to scuttle off and run a bath before I broke down and raided the fridge.

At nine o' clock that evening the massive terracotta pot arrived at its final destination – the centre of my well-scrubbed dining table. A golden, steaming bowlful of delicious, hearty southwestern cuisine with an aroma to resurrect the dead.

It's not a difficult recipe. It isn't even time consuming, you can get on with anything else you like whilst the cassoulet is quietly bubbling away. However, it is a needy dish. You can't just leave it and go out. You have to watch it; you have to be there for it, pampering it. Maybe that's why the people of this land love it so much. It's their baby, all theirs, and just you mind what you say about it.

★ ★ ★

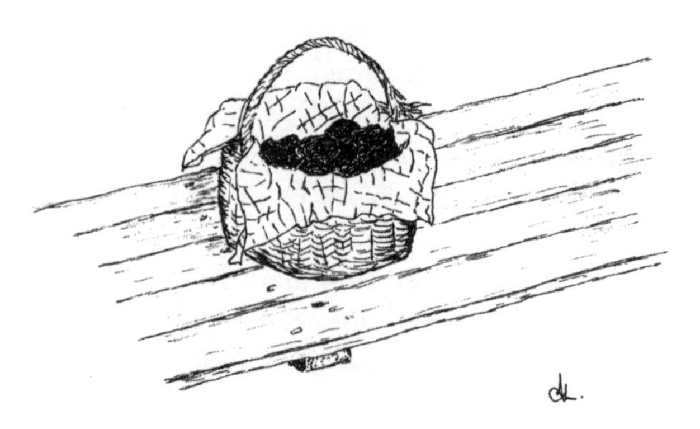

Black Gold Black Wine

Late February, and the winter work in the fields and vines is all but over for another year. Vineyards are immaculately groomed, the fields, bare of turnips and winter feed, stand dormant waiting for the warmth to creep back into the earth. There's a breathing space, a short lull before the mad scramble of spring. It is time to visit the famed market of Lalbenque, time for a little indulgence with the last of that most delectable and extravagant of winter treats, the black truffle.

Truffles are a mysterious commodity, a fungus that grows somewhat randomly on the roots of scrub oak and chestnut trees. They are utterly delicious of course, but so ridiculously expensive that the price you pay in the capitals of the world, in the winter of a bad year, almost rivals that of gold – well it feels that way anyway! This isn't just desirability, it's principally because they haven't yet been cultivated to any reliable degree; the vast majority are still found in the wild. There are several well-known areas, mainly in France and Italy, but the very best, it's universally agreed, is the utterly sublime and correspondingly expensive tuber melanosporum or black truffle, found mainly in the Perigord and Quercy, and sold straight from the soil in the Tuesday truffle market at Lalbenque – reputedly the largest of its kind in southwest France.

For the peasant with his pig or specially trained hound, it is like finding buried treasure beneath the trees, with the added bonus of being able to eat it. They call it the black diamond in these parts, but I feel gold would be a better metaphor. Apart from the value, this isn't a commodity that needs to be carefully mined and cut; with a bit of initiative, a good bit of stamina, a stick, a trained hound or a pig and a healthy dollop of luck, anyone can find an exciting dirt-covered nugget. There really is gold in these white-rock hills.

We decided to go along and see what all the fuss was about. I had a bowl of fresh brown eggs waiting in the kitchen with some beautiful crisp salad; a nice fat truffle would be the perfect accompaniment. The beloved patted his slender wallet nervously.

The little town of Lalbenque was sleepy as we approached at the highly unsociable hour of one-thirty. The population was cosily ensconced behind closed shutters, at lunch, and the streets were silent. As we rounded the bend to the village we were met by a welcome sight. A hand-painted sign declaring 'MARCHE DE TRUFFES' blocked the centre from encroaching traffic. We parked beside one of the pale grey stone houses and decided to get out and explore.

To be honest, it felt a bit like entering one of those one hoss towns that Clint Eastwood was forever swaggering around, booted, spurred and wrapped in a poncho. It was totally deserted, the sun beat down – it was five degrees below zero but you can't have everything – and the only sound was the swinging of the café door. Until, that is, we turned the corner into the main street – and there they were. A long line of half-frozen *paysans* just down from the hills, snugly wrapped against the bitter weather, berets on their heads, ancient boots on their feet. There must have been a hundred or so. In front of them was an elongated, rough, wooden bench of the sort you wouldn't consider fit for a school fête. On the bench before each *paysan* was a small basket lined with a tea towel or handkerchief – red and white seemed to be the approved colour scheme – and in each basket were between three and thirty lumpy black nuggets that looked, shall we say… unappetising.

A metre or so in front of the bench, a long rope held back a seething mass of buyers and a couple of hardy tourists brandishing digital cameras in frozen fingers. A heady aroma of *je ne sais quoi* pervaded the air. It's difficult to describe the scent of fresh truffles to those who've never experienced it. Mushroomy? Well, it isn't really. I would say it's sexy. The slightest trace of shellfish, maybe there's a hint of yeast and perhaps a whiff – just a faint whiff – of old knickers. But I assure you; the overall aroma is deliciously voluptuous.

It was a fascinating sight, but the market wasn't due to open until two-thirty and we still had forty-five minutes to go. My feet were already beginning to go into hibernation, and I began to realise the agonies Scott must have endured as he trudged the frozen wastes of the Antarctic with less and less hope of ever having warm feet again. We (I) decided to nip into the nearest café for an espresso and a welcoming blast of hot air.

The two cafés in the village centre were both advertising truffle laden specialities. *Omelettes aux Truffes*, *Porc Rôti aux Truffes* and even *Foie Gras aux Truffes.* Prices were as low as ever and I wondered how on earth they managed it. We sat at the bar, wrapped in steamy warmth, for some forty minutes or so, watching the locals devouring the last of the cheeses and polishing off several *digestifs*, whilst we discussed truffle bargaining tactics.

At two twenty-five the beloved decided the time had come to go out and do our stuff. We were a bit late. By this time, despite the penguin-friendly temperatures, the throng outside the rope had swollen to at least a couple of hundred and the chances of getting a prime position were slim, to put it mildly. Although the market had still not officially opened there seemed to be a hell of a lot of shady dealing going on. Baskets were handed over for sniffing, buyers ducked under the ropes, bulging wallets were produced and another paysan retired with a satisfied smirk. The beloved assumed his best narrow-eyed-gaucho look and plunged into the fray, attempting to imitate the smooth operators in expensive overcoats. We had decided we would approach the lady with just three truffles in her basket and try to persuade her to part with one of them. It wouldn't be easy; most of the buyers were clearly buying vast amounts. The *paysans* had weighed their contribution in advance and were offering them as job lots, and the going rate for the day was 700 euros a kilo, earth included.

Two-thirty came and went, the church bells chimed – somewhat tardily – and a little man with a hand-bell, a handful of leaflets and an official strut removed the rope and rang his bell loudly.

All hell let loose. The beloved was in there with the best of them, sniffing, squeezing and bargaining, but no deal. You either had to buy the whole lot – literally - or wait till the end and see if there are any lots unsold, in which case you might be able to buy one or two loose. We waited. My feet went back into hibernation and the chaos at the benches gradually began to wane as the choicest lots were quickly sold to the men in camel coats. An old *paysan* with a small but good-looking basketful was beginning to assume a mournful expression. This was obviously the time. The beloved drew a fistful of euros and he succumbed to temptation, cautiously surrendering a moist, fat truffle.

We sped back to the car in heady triumph. Actually the beloved sped; I hobbled. I could no longer feel my knees.

That evening I concocted my own version of the classic *omelette aux truffes*. The omelettes were fat and slightly runny in the centre, and the sublime, inimitable scent of truffles permeated the kitchen. We ate them with crisp, juicy salad, a baguette, warm from the bakery in Albas, and a jug of rich, dark Cahors from the vineyards behind the house. It was worth cold feet.

*

A good, strong bottle of Cahors wine is the classic accompaniment to virtually any truffle-studded dish. It's a marriage of convenience, as both ingredients grow in the sparse Quercy hillsides, and like many such marriages it works fabulously.

The Cahors vineyards have a long, distinguished but somewhat chequered history. Originally planted by the conquering Romans at the beginning of the first century AD, they were amongst the first ever planted commercially in France. The thin, chalky soil and astute choice of grape variety produced a powerful and heady wine, immediately successful in Imperial circles, they were known even then as the black wines. Pick up a glass of well-matured Cahors and you'll see why; it's one of the richest, darkest wines in the world.

Unfortunately for Cahors, the Roman Empire was also rather successful, and spreading so fast that all land possible was needed to grow wheat to feed the new citizens. France was to be its breadbasket and the vines would have to go. Not only that, but the vignerons in Italy weren't all that amused that their Imperial masters had taken a shine to a wine produced – Bacchus forgive them – in France! It wasn't until the third century that some of the vineyards were restored by that far-sighted epicurean, Emperor Probus, a fact still celebrated today by one of the well-known Châteaux. One of their classic wines,

100% Malbec, strong, tannic, beautifully rounded and delicious, is named Prince Probus, in his honour.

For many hundreds of years the wines of the Quercy region were well known as some of the very best in the world. Long before Bordeaux had become a household name, Cahors wines were being sold to the rich and exalted. It is said that whilst Burgundy produced wines for the men of the Roman legions, Cahors was reserved for the officers.

Later on the Church enthusiastically embraced it. St Didier, an early local bishop, patronised it zealously and caused its fame to spread. This well-connected local boy happened to be King Dagobert's treasurer and it's entirely due to his efforts that Cahors began to rise from the ashes of medieval warfare to rebuild both its town and its reputation as a world-class purveyor of fine wines. Still later the delicious vintages of Cahors were reserved for the popes. Jacques Duèze, another homegrown cleric – who became Pope John XXII – was particularly partial and spent a great deal of his time promoting the nectar of his home town from his papal palaces in Avignon and Châteauneuf. He even had the vines planted there and greatly improved the wines of the area – ever heard of Châteauneuf-du-Pape? But of course you can't produce a Cahors black wine in Provence, any more than you could produce a light Provençal rosé in Cahors.

For centuries afterwards the famous black wines graced the dining tables and refectory tables of the Christian world. By the time the Bourbon kings came to the throne Cahors wine was being transported down the river Lot to the great trading port of Bordeaux, where it was rumoured to be mixed with their lighter wines to bolster them up a little (but you must never say so) before being exported to the finest cellars in the world. Since then the vineyards have resisted wars, droughts, floods, forest fires and even revolutions, but at the end of the nineteenth century another, even more devastating catastrophe occurred. Not an emperor's whim this time, but a parasite. The ravages of phylloxera comprehensively wiped out all the vines of the Quercy. Wholesale replanting began in the early decades of the twentieth century, only to be thwarted by nature once again in 1956. The great freeze of February '56 was the worst on record and once more wiped out much of the vine-stock. The weary vignerons re-planted yet again, using the rich, tannic Malbec – or Auxerrois as it's known locally – as the backbone of their wine, with perhaps a little Merlot for fruity modern tastes. The emperors wouldn't have had any old chariot with that, they liked their wine strong, dark and unadorned by any such unnecessary fripperies as toasty bouquet or fruity flavour. The Russian Tsars agreed wholeheartedly with this viewpoint. Peter the Great reputedly used Cahors almost exclusively, not only for his dining table but also because he claimed the high tannic content would cure his ulcer. More recently scientists investigating the famous French Paradox – why the people of southwest France live such long lives – have discovered something else. It's now widely accepted that a couple of glasses of red wine a night has a very healthy effect on the cardio-vascular system, all a matter of phenols apparently. But which wines have the most phenols? Cabernet Sauvignon? Gamay? No. The grape with the gold medal was Malbec, and the two highest scoring were Madiran and Cahors, both from southwest France. Well, well.

In 1971 the French government finally recognised this jewel in their non-existent crown, and granted Cahors wine A.O.C. status. Since then there's been no looking back, the wines have gone from strength to strength. They are still dry and dark, but they are also warm, rich and complex, in fact quite delectable and not yet too expensive or exclusive. But – just a whisper in your private ear – it won't be long before the rediscovery of this black jewel is neither local nor even national, but global.

Meanwhile, back in the Quercy the locals nurse their secret. Cahors is one of the finest wines in the world. It will keep for many years, slowly maturing, developing more depth and flavour, getting better and better.

Rich, dry and as tannic as any Tsar could wish, it may not be to everyone's taste, but if you have a four course dinner laid before you in the frozen depths of winter, beginning with truffles, followed by some fat goose or duck, padded with good bread and ending with several strong cheeses and a *tarte aux noix*, there is nothing in the world to beat it.

⋆

A couple of weeks after our successful truffle initiation I happened to bump into one of my elderly vigneron neighbours, whilst out for my afternoon constitutional. And it was brought home to me, in the simplest way, just why the increasingly popular wines of this region are still so rare and so very difficult to find elsewhere.

"Eh, ma petite?" He ground to a halt in anticipation of a long and enjoyable discourse. His conversation tends to run like that, peppered with *'ehs', 'ahs' 'behs'* and *'poufs'* and he gets very much more animated if he has access to a comely female to keep the testosterone pumping – or so I fear – and lubricate his agile imagination.

He removed his roll-up courteously before fondling me with evident enjoyment on the cheeks. He treats me rather as if I'm a cross between favoured granddaughter and bit-on-the-side, odd but not unpleasant.

I told him I was very well and asked if the pruning was all over for the season. He re-inserted his cigarette, the better to use his hands for illustrative purposes, and began to explain the shortcomings of some of the lazy old fools round here, who don't bother to prune their vines before the warm weather. His, naturally, were all done weeks ago. He pulled absent-mindedly at the spiral of soggy rope hanging from one pocket of his hunting jacket, and fingered the head of what looked suspiciously like a dead partridge hanging from the other. He's a respected man in these parts, head of a numerous family that, between them, own a large and productive slice of our valley, although less than a quarter of it is now laid to vines; the rest is just scrub oak and pine forest, beautiful but not very lucrative. Maybe it had once been cultivated? I asked him curiously; I'd been wondering for some time just why there were so many half-collapsing stone terraces all over the hillsides.

"Oui, oui, oui!" It's curious the way an elderly Frenchman's mouth alters over the years, so that he can speak – after a fashion – out of one side, whilst holding his fag firmly in place with the other. Monsieur gave me a demonstration of this arcane practice. He drew a wide map with his arm; in his great grandfather's day nearly all of it had been vineyards – puff – only enough woodland left for the la chasse and to keep the fires going – puff. But then there was the phylloxera disaster and after that, he could still remember, the terrible frosts of fifty-six. He sighed and puffed deeply, *"une vraie catastrophe,* the vines were never replanted."

I nodded, but I was more than a little intrigued. Why weren't they replanted? After all these wines aren't just ordinary old plonk are they? They're valuable. If he and his family were to replant the whole valley – and maybe invest in some more up to date equipment – they could make a small fortune.

He chuckled, coughed, puffed and raised his hands to shoulder level. What would they do with a fortune? After all, they lived in a lovely old farmhouse in one of the most beautiful places in France – so he'd been told – he'd never actually been further than Toulouse and he certainly had no wish to travel anywhere more exotic. They had the best food and indisputably the best wine in the world, rivers of it, with plenty left over to sell to the *négociants* and plenty more for friends and neighbours. Why make more work? He'd have no time for the boules tournaments.

I looked at him with increased respect. He's absolutely right of course. Our modern world is so obsessed with making money, almost for the sake of it, that we rarely stop to consider our real needs and wants.

He tapped the side of his nose conspiratorially as if he'd just imparted the secret of life, which I suppose in a sense he had. Then he whipped out his cigarette to say his farewells and enjoy himself with my cheeks a second time.

"Bonne soirée ma petite." His old walnut-stained face cracked into a virtually toothless grin, and whistling for his venerable, arthritic hound he kicked at the dead leaves and strode off to inspect his pristine vines.

*

Almost overnight - a suddenness that can leave a pale Englishwoman gasping in wonder - spring arrived in the Quercy. The willows dripped with green, almonds turned their pale pink blossoms to the new sunlight and riots of blackthorn lit the hedgerows. At the bottom of the valley the Lot was in full flood, the trees at Castelfranc were swimming under water and the whole countryside had taken on a green haze. In the markets the *jonquille* sellers had arrived in force; little old ladies in tight pinnies and ancient shawls, their venerable faces collapsed with the weight of years, their black olive eyes as lively as ever and their wits even livelier.

"Un beau bouquet, Madame!" One of them snared me on the way in and hung on to my sleeve. *"Deux euros – ou trois pour cinq!"*

I didn't really need them; they're always sold in full bloom and would be dead in two days. She deftly wrapped three bunches in damp newspaper and held them out. On the other hand… I fumbled for a five-euro note, placed them cheerfully at the edge of my basket and moved swiftly on. Every other stall was overflowing with luscious young vegetables, asparagus and *aillet*, tiny, sweet carrots and bunches of *ciboulette*. It was nearing lunchtime and the sun was hot, muscular arms were bared and spirits were high. I bought a crusty *baguette de campagne,* queued for half a *poulet roti* and managed to restrain myself from buying more than the required amount of fresh young salad from the reassuringly grubby fingers of M. Dubois.

As I climbed back into the trusty Passat and crawled back up into the hills I noticed little scratches of lemon yellow on the verges; further up they became darns amongst the thin new grass. Cowslips, the first of the season. Before long there would be sheets of them, spread joyfully over banks, between vineyards and into pastures, bringing the sunlight down to earth. A little further on I spied a purple patch among the oaks, like a flung imperial mantle. It was a huge spread of violets, the famed flower of Toulouse.

I had all the windows down by this time. The air was soft and warm and the heady scents of spring wafted through the car. Above me I could hear the buzzards cry as they wheeled in the rising thermals and below, on the white rocks by the roadside, lizards pumped new life into their cold winter bodies.

I knew exactly how they felt. Spring is short in these southern lands. Winter had been banished to the frozen north, and the long, hot summer was just round the next hairpin. Bliss.

★ ★ ★

The Fabulous Fête Du Vin

The largest wine festival in the Cahors region is set in one of its tiniest villages. Albas is an arresting sight, especially when viewed from the river, which is easier than one would expect as it has its own little bridge. It's a single span, one track, perilously narrow affair, but it's still a bridge. The village is a charming and tightly packed cluster of houses, constructed entirely of local stone, dominated by the church and wedged precariously into a rocky cleft on the almost sheer left bank of the river. The bishops of Cahors once had a country residence here and it's always played a prominent role in the wine trade. It is, therefore, not only venerable but was once richly endowed, boasting a very large church for such an exiguous community. The population is normally pretty stable at around five hundred – that's if you include all the surrounding farms and tiny hamlets – but on one particular day each May it swells to several thousand. It's the day of the annual *fête du vin* and the whole village bows in worship of the grape and gives itself up to the pleasures of the table. It also throws open its hospitable gates to all comers, and come they do, in droves.

"Last year we are having six thousand people," the portly mayor confided to me, his amiable face the colour of spilt wine, "this year maybe more?"

The thought of six thousand inebriated people crammed into little Albas was arresting to say the very least; surely they'd be falling into the river? I decided I'd better go along to see what it was all about and what measures had been taken to prevent a watery end.

Festivals of this magnitude are all day affairs, and this one started with a special ten o'clock mass in the church, with all the local children dressed in period costume. This was followed by a huge and appropriately boozy lunch for those who felt they could cope with it. Five fabulous courses had been prepared by one of Cahors' top chefs, strictly limited, rather expensive, definitely booked well in advance and absolutely not for the faint-hearted. After the initial feasting the true business of the day got under way. Eight local vineyards – and one guest *domaine* from the western edge of the Cahors AOC area – were offering *dégustations* of their 2003 vintage, each in one of the cool, dark cellars hewn from the very rock under the village houses, hundreds of years ago. With the exception of the main thoroughfare, all the streets had been closed to the public and screened with hundreds of yards of bamboo matting – to ensure no one squeezed in for a free tipple I suppose. This meant that the entire northern side of the village, the oldest and largest bit, containing both the mairie and the church, was out of bounds for the duration – unless you were a bona-fide resident naturally.

On the far side of the mairie the cliffs plunge a good fifty feet to the river.You'd have to be pretty desperate for a drink to force an entry by that route, so I decided I'd have to use the only viable way in, through a roped off walkway, after payment of a larcenous twelve euros. For this princely sum, I received a small glass engraved with the official logo *'le bon air est dans les caves'* and this year's festival date.After acceptance of the glass I had to submit to having my hand rubber-stamped by an elderly dame wearing a dazzling Marie-Antoinette style wig. Now I was at liberty to wander up and down entirely at my leisure, visit all the *caves* and taste all the delicious nectar produced by one of the hottest summers for years.At least I could in theory. In practice there are only so many tastings the tummy can take before the eyes begin to cross; I reached this stage in about the fifth *cave*, and found myself propped against the cool stone, grinning vacuously at one of the local 'beautiful people' who hadn't quite made it to San Francisco but was nevertheless wearing lilac flowers in his hair. Next door, through an ancient brick arch, a venerable jazz band – average age sixty – was resonating with fascinating rhythm. I departed in search of a sop for the alcohol before things got completely out of control.

Naturally this contingency had been well provided for. One could purchase a sandwich either of *foie gras* or local, salty Rocamadour goat's cheese from a vast pile at two impromptu snack bars.Then there was the village restaurant, fully booked, fit to burst and doing a roaring trade. Lastly, if you were feeling really hungry, you could join the official supper party, another twelve euros, but well worth it judging from the enticing aromas wafting up from the vast marquee. Places were strictly limited to twelve hundred. I bought a Rocamadour sandwich and rather rashly went in search of *cave* number six.

"Madame Lawrence, *quelle surprise!*" It was the *maire*, taking his social duties very seriously indeed, even after the prolonged and doubtless quite exhausting lunch. He's a man with a figure that in every way befits his exalted status. Official receptions, lunches, dinners – so long and arduous – had taken their inevitable toll. He was proudly sporting the vast vigneron's campaign medal on his curving shirtfront and wore a permanent wide smile on his face.

"Monsieur Pezat, un beau jour pour la fête n'est pas?"

"Oh, it always is," he maintained airily, putting his hand on his gong and lunging for my ears. "Have you met my wife?" I had, several times, but since he'd obviously forgotten I thought it politic not to say so.

"Enchanté Madame," I murmured, but at that point we were interrupted by a march of a dozen or so huge, hairy looking characters, dressed in traditional Breton costumes with lace headdresses and playing Celtic pipes. Bizarre! I noticed their lipstick had been pretty well smudged too. Obviously I wasn't the only one having trouble with the number of *caves*.

The wines really were extremely palatable and becoming mysteriously more so with every glass. Maybe the guests had a slight edge on the locals I thought judiciously, making my way back to their *cave* for a second glass in the interests of fair play. But after all Clos Triguedina is one of the great Cahors *domaines*, and this was a privileged tasting of their expensive blue ribbon wine, Prince Probus. It should have been good. I gave it a second, more thorough tasting. It was very good indeed and could only get better. One for the *cave* at home I decided, rashly ignoring the elevated price that matches its lofty reputation.

It was nearing seven o'clock by this time and the streets were thronged. The pre-dinner crowd had arrived for a lingering aperitif before rushing home for their usual four courses of splendid, home-cooked, Quercynoise cuisine. Laughter echoed round the ancient streets and conversation levels notched up a decibel or so. The farmers and vignerons began to trickle in from the fields and vineyards, and in front of the church steps three, rather self-conscious nuns blinked at the crowds as if they could hardly believe their eyes. They didn't seem to be carrying glasses I noticed. Hiding behind a group of giant yuccas I subjected them to a critical gaze, were they in costume or were they really nuns? Unable to tell, I decided I'd probably had more than enough wine; it was time to bring on the coffee and cake.

The party-piece of this grand show was a gigantic *gâteau* made by one of the region's premier *patissiers*; fifteen hundred portions of gooey indulgence, a masterpiece in anybody's book. It wasn't to be served until after the dinner though, so I decided to eschew the final revelries and go home to nurse my embryo hangover.

Fighting my way back up the winding streets, I fended off the masses and admired the incredibly intricate paper sculptures that decorated the ancient stone walls. A wonderful dancing pink pig, two metres high and the improbable official emblem of this year's fête, adorned one of the little alleyways. Bacchus himself held court in another and several more sculptures of a vinous nature were suspended high over our heads.

In one of the blind alleys a collection of extremely interesting looking persons – a sort of cross between the inhabitants of Scooby-doo's Mystery Machine and the hard-core party animals at Woodstock – were blowing some sweet notes my way and scraping their dreadlocks on the cobbles as they did so. I listened for a few heady minutes, and for a split second I could almost imagine myself travelling through Europe in the back of an orange and white Volkswagen van, sharing the bread and wine, growing my hair to impossible lengths and lying naked on the beach. But I can't play the guitar – or indeed any other musical instrument – and it would possibly mean sharing a bivouac with the gentleman playing the sax. I gave him a sideways glance. No, I couldn't do it.

Meanwhile the village children were gathering in happy little knots, enjoying the late sunshine and the prospect of a late night out. One of them approached me with a courteous half bow and introduced himself with great aplomb. He was a friend of my daughter, he informed me, and he'd like to take her to the cinema if I'd no objections. I hedged slightly, spread my hands, shrugged and stood awkwardly on one leg – which wasn't terribly prudent under the circumstances – but I was a little taken aback to say the least.

They were both ten years old.

⋆

A fortnight or so after the local vignerons annual party, I happened to catch up with one of our nearest and most garrulous neighbours, out amongst his vines in the sweltering heat. Monsieur the Elder waded out to greet me, slapping the flies and wiping the sweat from his face in anticipation of a hearty embrace and a nice gossip.

"But what is this you are wearing *ma petite?*" He enquired, peering at my bare arms. It was more a question of what I wasn't wearing, and although he made it quite clear that he was grateful for the unexpected enhancement of his view, I must be aware that my health would certainly suffer. I should go home immediately and don something more decorous. Failing that, he might be willing to lend me his well-worn, sweaty, extremely grimy cardigan.

I produced a bottle of Ambre Solaire and tried to explain that I really wasn't in any danger of sunburn.

"Bof!" He waved his cotton hat at me disgustedly. "For the tourists only! You live here now, you must start to behave as one

of us or you could be very ill." He spat out the end of his roll-up and ground it with his heel. "Your health is important, this you must understand!"

Now, I'm all for behaving as one when it comes to adhering to local customs, attending local events, eating local food and drinking the fruit of my cross neighbour's labours. But I draw the line at wearing his ragged old cardigan. And that wasn't the end of the diatribe. I had even had the temerity to put my hair up, thereby exposing my neck and half my back, not only to the sun's lethal rays but also to the gaze of the youths of this up-to-now uncorrupted valley. Had I no sense of decency? He shook his head despairingly. It was all very well to expose my charms to such sober (sober?) and mature persons as he, but his grandson over there, he pointed to an entirely unheeding, bronzed figure toiling in the distance. Had I no idea of the effect such an expanse of womanly flesh would have? I hadn't and actually I would rather liked to have known, but this really didn't seem to be the appropriate moment to say so. I promised to go home and cover up *tout de suite* and made a mental note to keep a shirt in the car to prevent further corruption of the valley's youth.

It was only when I got home and was staggering in and out with the fruits of my own labours in the market that I remembered I needed some more wine. That was why I'd taken the little road that leads past my neighbour's vineyard in the first place. The Ambre Solaire versus woolly cardigan argument had driven it out of my head. I sighed; unless dinner was going to be dry – unthinkable – I'd have to go back. What's more, I'd have to put some more clothes on.

The temperatures were nudging thirty-five in the shade, but neighbourliness undoubtedly had to come first, besides I wasn't likely to be endowed with any wine unless I complied with the unwritten local rules. I employed the antiperspirant, flung on a linen shirt, let my hair down and jumped back in the car to reconcile my differences with Monsieur the Elder. Hopefully he'd approve of my more decorous appearance and allow me to purchase a few litres of the splendid vintage of 2003, before they bottled it and it was no longer available *en vrac.*

One of the many perks of living amongst vineyards is the ability to buy wine loose or, *en vrac.* It's the same stuff that one buys in bottles but without the fancy packaging and therefore at a fraction of the price. Of course the smaller domaines just don't have storage room for dozens of vintages, so when the *vendange* is over they generally have to clean out the previous year's barrels and either sell the wine to the co-operative or bottle it and sell it to the *négociants.* If you stand in a queue at one of the local supermarkets in this area, you'll see what I mean. All these shops are thoroughly clued up to the tourist trade and well aware of the huge potential of their precious black wine. There are often as many as fifty different Cahors domaines and vintages on display. From May to October you'll see them diving off the shelves into hot trolleys. Now just take a peek at the customers. They are all visitors, no self-respecting local would buy his wine bottled, let alone from a supermarket. That's a place to go for soap, floor cloths and a new broom handle.

Having said that, we're just a tad guilty of the practice ourselves. We shouldn't do it, it's far more expensive, and with vineyards literally on our doorstep it's not exactly upholding the commerce of our valley. But it's terribly difficult not to succumb to a couple of bottles of a rather good vintage that you're quite certain will compliment your roast duck to perfection. It isn't that we don't like to visit the vineyards, we do, it's a highly enjoyable education, but it's outrageously time consuming. No true Frenchman will let you go without observing the formalities of ritual kissing, enquiries about health, family and friends, followed by desultory conversation concerning local events, weather and politics. Usually they'll lure you to a lingering aperitif – if it happens to be just before lunch or dinner – a quick dégustation if it doesn't. It can add well over an hour to a shopping trip.

Back at the vineyard Monsieur the Elder, having approved the change in my apparel, directed his daughter-in-law to the cave to squirt five litres of the 2003 into a plastic bidon for my delectation. He poured the aperitifs himself, and pushing back his cotton hat to scratch his head, he asked courteously after my family. I told him about my daughter's close brush with the back row of a cinema. He nodded,

"He is a good boy, Clement, she refused him did she?" I was a little flustered by his phlegmatic response. "She's a bit young anyway," I ventured, "but yes, thankfully, she did refuse him."

He nodded again and examined the inky depths of his glass before switching subjects without warning and observing portentously,

"Good Cahors wine, there is none finer. Good sunshine," he waved his hand vaguely at the sky, "and the fat of the goose. You'll live to be a hundred!" He took a long gulp of the former, smacked his lips and raised his glass. *"Le raisaing!"*

I'll drink to that.

* * *

LADY ELEANOR

Yellow broom flowers brushed past my legs as I wandered down through my wildly overgrown garden to inspect the almond trees. *Planta genista.* The mass of lemon-yellow blossom reminded me of the southern princess whose life became entangled with it, whose very name is inexorably linked to it.

The women in this area of the world have always been strong. For many hundreds of years they had to hold families together whilst their men went off to fight crusades, defend their villages against marauding armies or even accompany the rich and devout on pilgrimages. But there is one who stands gracious head and lovely shoulders above the common horde. Was she the inspiration for the haunting Lindisfarne song? I have no idea, but she was certainly the inspiration for many of its precursors, the famed but largely forgotten medieval ballads. She was, and in many respects she still is, the first lady of Aquitaine, one of the very few women in the medieval world who were to become movers and shakers. She was probably born at the Château d'Ombrieres outside medieval Bordeaux, just a hundred miles or so from where I was standing, knee-deep in the shrub that was to name the dynasty she founded.

Eleonore – or Aliénor in Occitan – became Duchess of Aquitaine in her own right on the untimely death of her father, Guillaume X. Having led a life devoted rather more to the gratification of the flesh than the feeding of the soul; the Duke decided the time had come to embark upon that most popular of medieval hikes, a pilgrimage to Santiago de Compostella. Until he had obtained forgiveness for his many sins, God, he felt quite sure, would never grant him a son to replace his much-mourned heir, who had never gained a firm grip on life and died around the same time as his mother, some five years earlier. Plans for re-marriage had somehow been thwarted and the Duke had become convinced that the hand of God was involved in all this. Before making any more attempts to marry and beget another son he must mend his ways and make atonement for his hitherto somewhat licentious life.

Guillaume set off, clad in traditional pilgrim's garb, with the scallop shell around his neck, at the onset of winter – a little unwisely perhaps – leaving his fourteen year old daughter to rule in his stead. Not surprisingly, he never returned. He died at Santiago, on Good Friday the following year, and was buried in the cathedral, beneath the altar.

At that time, Aquitaine – land of the rivers – was a huge domain, stretching from the fertile plains of the Loire valley to the high peaks of the Pyrenees, and from the Atlantic coast to the spiny uplands of the Massif Central. Although the Duchy theoretically owed allegiance to the French crown, in practice Aquitaine was as large as medieval France and considerably richer, so the Dukes behaved pretty much as they pleased.

All this meant that overnight the spirited and beautiful Eleonore had become the most desirable heiress in Europe. If nothing else, however, Guillaume had anticipated this little wrinkle in his plan. Before he departed for his ill-fated trip he arranged for Eleanore's betrothal to the Dauphin of France. A most desirable alliance for all – except the leading players, unfortunately – giving Eleonore protection and France the rich, rolling lands of Aquitaine.

Actually Eleonore's presence in France had been felt long before the fateful pilgrimage. Guillaume IX, known as the troubadour, was her paternal grandfather and his elaborate court was one of the first to introduce the idea of courtly love into the mundane business of dutiful marriage. Eleonore and her adoring younger sister, Petronilla, were apt pupils indeed. Troubadours sat at their feet and praised their beauty before either could possibly have reached an age to have attained it. By the time she was thirteen there were few powerful families in Europe who hadn't heard of the charms of Eleonore of Aquitaine. Beautiful, (this is an assumption based on the reports of contemporary chroniclers because, strangely, the only reliable image of her still in existence is the elegant effigy on her tomb at Fontevrault Abbey) she was also accomplished, spirited – without the faintest shadow of a doubt – and heiress to vast lands, numerous titles and a fortune. Therefore, as soon as the King of France, unkindly but truthfully nicknamed Louis the Fat, heard of the events in Santiago he arranged for the immediate marriage of his son and heir to this most luscious of plums. Eleanore was more than ready for the marriage bed but unfortunately her shy little prince was not. He was Louis' second son, his first, the somewhat precocious Philippe, having died some years earlier after being trampled by a herd of swine in the noisome streets of Paris. As was the custom in those times, young Louis had originally been destined for the church. He was steeped in the sanctity of sacred matters, a monk in everything but name and bitterly resented the weighty mantle of responsibility that was now his.

For a little while the outstanding beauty and vitality of his young bride helped to overcome his natural reticence, and he fell deeply and helplessly in love, whilst on Eleonore's part, the role of princess was one she played to absolute perfection. Within a month, however, Louis the Fat succumbed to his infirmities and his reluctant son was proclaimed Louis VII. Eleonore of Aquitaine had become Queen of France.

For Louis, his father's demise made his marriage even more difficult. Struggling to come to grips with affairs of state, he had little time to devote to his passionate young queen and Eleonore was not at all used to such indifference. For some years she subdued her natural spirit and personality, but it couldn't last. She was unhappy in the cold and damp of Paris and yearned for the warm breezes and kind climate of her native southwest – and who could blame her? Her inexperienced and socially clumsy husband left her even colder. Something had to give; she had to find an outlet for her frustrated energies. This was the twelfth century, however, a time when European women owed absolute obedience to whichever man happened to have authority over them; firstly their fathers and then generally their husbands. Eleanore was not at liberty to pursue her own life; she would have to find a cause, an adventure that would interest and excite Louis. No easy task.

Her chance came in 1146 with the famous sermon of Abbe Bernard at Vezelay. Both she and Louis would take holy vows to deliver Jerusalem from the infidel, and join the Second Crusade.

With her characteristic single-mindedness and intense drive, Eleonore set about recruiting crusaders and selecting the ladies who would accompany her. It was to be the greatest enterprise of her life and she was determined to enjoy it. That the purpose of all this frenetic activity was to wrench Jerusalem from Muslim hands, thus bestowing salvation on all those taking part, was, in all probability a satisfying bonus. It's far more likely that the real reason for Eleonore's personal crusade was thrilling adventure.

So it was that in 1147 the Queen bade farewell to the cloistered life of Paris, said a tender goodbye to the three-year old Princess Marie and set off for Constantinople. At Metz her pious husband and a brilliant cavalcade of Christian soldiers joined her. They travelled triumphantly across Europe, a hundred thousand strong, with the golden fleur-de-lys of France flying in the wind beside the red cross of Christianity. It must have been an awe-inspiring sight.

They were away for several years, and during that time, despite the birth of another daughter, Alix, it became obvious to all that Louis and Eleanore had become estranged. There are many rumours as to what the spirited queen got up to during that time; that she took a lover, and perhaps more than one, seems quite certain. One of those to whom she undoubtedly became rather too close was Raymond of Antioch, her own uncle. Another was the Saracen leader, Saladin. For Eleonore this was all heady romance, the stuff of her grandfather's famed courts of love and the breath of life. For Louis it had become a waking nightmare. When they finally returned to France – in separate ships – Eleonore began to sue for an annulment, pleading as an excuse the close blood tie between them. Louis resisted, argued and pleaded, but he was no match, and sadly had never been any match for the determined Eleonore. When his friend and spiritual advisor, that kindly and wise old owl, Abbe Suger, died, Louis had no one left to turn to and his resistance began to crumble.

It was during this stormy period in her life that Eleonore first met Geoffrey of Anjou, known as Plantagenet because of the sprig of broom – that same *planta genista* which grows so abundantly in my half-wild garden – which he invariably wore in his hat. He was also known as The Fair, a soubriquet that probably explains Eleonore's immediate interest in him. However, no matter his undoubted charms, the scales dropped from her eyes once she met his vital and energetic seventeen-year-old son, and from that moment on she desired no other man.

Henry of Anjou, also surnamed Plantagenet, had a glittering future before him. He was already Duke of Normandy; he was heir not only to the lands of Anjou and Maine, but also direct heir to the English crown. He needed sons of his own as soon as possible and he needed a lady to be his queen.

There was no woman in the whole of Christendom who could fill this role to more dazzling effect than Eleonore. She was beautiful and she was an experienced woman, no simpering girl. She was possessed of vast lands and enormous wealth and, on top of all of this, she was endlessly fascinating. Henry was entranced. Despite the difference in their ages – Eleonore was eleven years his senior – it was love at first sight. The only bar to their future happiness was Louis, and when had Eleonore ever considered Louis?

In March 1152 the marriage between the King and Queen of France was annulled on the grounds of consanguinity – that supremely useful royal marriage escape clause – and Eleonore slipped quietly away from the grimy, chilly streets of Paris to her own warm lands.

She must have been ecstatic with relief. The only slight edge to her euphoria lay in parting with her two young daughters, Marie and Alix. They were princesses of France and would necessarily remain in Paris. But neither were babies any more and their need for her was waning, it was no longer enough to hold Eleonore back. Besides, she had other matters on her mind.

Two months later, on May 18th, a sunny Whit Sunday, Eleonore, Duchess of Aquitaine rode to the cathedral in her capital of Poitiers and was quietly united to Henry Plantagenet, Duke of Normandy.

It was a love affair that was to change the course of both English and French history and was directly responsible for the close ties this rural region of modern day France has with England. Eleonore and Henry would now need all their considerable wits and strength to fight for their right to the English throne. No couple were better able to do so.

At that time the English succession was in a complicated mess. Stephen of Blois – who had married Adela, the Conqueror's youngest daughter – sat uneasily on the throne, however the crown should by rights have gone to Matilda, known as the Empress, the only daughter and direct heir of Henry I. She was also the wife of Geoffrey of Anjou and Henry's mother. Matilda was a strong woman herself; like her daughter-in-law she had been twice married. As a child she had been betrothed to the Emperor of Germany and married very young. He gave her a title she enjoyed enormously and never relinquished. But unlike Eleonore she had no charm at all, only a stubborn arrogance, and it was that arrogance that had lost her the throne. She realised that now, and was determined to regain it for her son. With his determined mother to fight his corner and his powerful and charismatic wife by his side there was nothing Henry could not achieve. When Stephen died in October 1154, he immediately laid claim to the throne, and on 19th December that same year he was crowned King Henry II of England at Westminster Abbey.

Eleonore of Aquitaine had become a queen for the second time. From that moment on England and France were entwined for better or worse.

By this time Eleanor, as she was now known, had already given Henry two sons; William, who died young, and Henry, later to be unwisely crowned within his father's lifetime and known as the Young King. She was also soon to present him with a daughter, Matilda.

Life at the English court wasn't exactly peaceful, with two strong and colourful characters such as Henry and Eleanor, peace could hardly be expected. Part of the problem was that their realm was so vast, stretching from the Scottish borders to the Pyrenees. Henry was constantly away, settling disputes, fighting battles and dealing with skirmishes. In his absence someone must act as regent, a role Eleanor relished. She was also forever dealing with the results of Henry's virility, which would have made constant travel not only uncomfortable but also dangerous. There was no woman who could take Eleanor's place in Henry's life, no woman who would ever take her place on the throne, but his bed was another matter. Henry was a passionate man and, despite his love for Eleanor, there was a constant string of mistresses.

Despite her past infidelities, Eleanor was a romantic at heart; she expected men to fall in love with her, it was ingrained in her. The troubadours of her childhood, where she had reigned supreme as queen of the courts of love, had conditioned her to expect nothing less than absolute devotion. Life, it seemed, wasn't quite like that. She'd had a weak man who adored her, now she had a strong one who certainly loved her but was not averse to taking his pleasure elsewhere if she were not around. It was a matter of preference.

Eleanor would take Henry.

Incredibly she bore him eight children, and on the 8th September 1157 an event occurred that would ease the pain of Henry's philandering. She gave birth to her third son, who was to become a legend in both England and France and the sweet-core of Eleanor's heart. She named him Richard, later to be known as *Coeur de Lion.*

By the time Eleanor was forty-five she had given birth to ten children, five sons and five daughters. After the birth of John, her last child, Eleanor spent more and more time in her native lands, either in Poitiers or Bordeaux, reinstating the fantastic and romantic courts of love, ruling her devoted people, negotiating marriage contracts for her various relatives and aiding and abetting her sons to revolt against their father. Henry's passion for her had long burnt out; they had been married for nearly twenty years and, although he would never commit the ultimate folly of divorcing her – or more accurately, Aquitaine – as poor Louis had done, he no longer sought her company. In 1174 Henry actually had her imprisoned and held her captive, luxuriously of course, for the next fifteen years, until his death in 1189. He was fifty-six. Eleanor was, by this time, sixty-eight, but still as vivacious and elegant as ever. As her eldest son William had died as an infant and Henry, the adventurous Young King had died at Martel castle after a disgraceful ransacking of the holy shrine at Rocamadour; the new King of England was to be her favourite child. Noble, handsome, inherently chivalrous Richard. She was immediately released and given a new zest for life. The Crusader King had made her regent of England.

At this time Richard was absolutely committed to – some might say obsessed with – the family hobby, in his case the third Crusade. Jerusalem was once more in the hands of the infidel, and like his beloved mother before him, Richard had vowed to win back the holy city for Christendom or die in the attempt. His reign, his constant battles with his brother, John and the state to which England was reduced by his continued absence is well documented history, and through tales such as Ivanhoe and Robin Hood has passed into myth and legend. Unfortunately Richard had little time for women. He remained unmarried until, once more, Eleanor took a hand. In 1191, at the incredible age of seventy, she travelled out to Naples taking with her a young princess, Berengaria of Navarre.

Richard and Berengaria were married in Cyprus on the

12th May and she was immediately crowned Queen of England. That it was a love-match actually seems quite possible, but Richard was far too engrossed in the Crusade to spare too much thought for his new bride and, although one must assume the marriage was consummated, they were never blessed with children. Prince John remained heir presumptive to the English throne and Richard continued his never-ending quest throughout Europe and especially in France.

In April 1199 he was struck by an arrow whilst holding siege to the town of Chalus in the Limousin. The wound quickly became gangrenous, and Richard realised that he was dying. He immediately sent for Eleanor, who is said to have travelled *ventre à terre* to his side. She arrived on the 6th April and Richard died in her arms that very day. His body was buried, at his own request, at his father's feet in the Abbey of Fontevrault and his lion heart was interred in the cathedral at Rouen.

Eleanor was broken-hearted and retired to her beloved Aquitaine. Even in her grief she was still energetic, still cementing marriage alliances, guiding policy and embellishing her lands with the many different cultures and foods of her travels. One of the most famous of these was the walnut. It is said that it was she who first planted the walnut groves of the Quercy and Perigord. But even she, always so strong and vital, couldn't live forever and with the untimely death of the Lion Heart, the heart went out of her too. She decided to enter the abbey of Fontevrault as a nun. There she could remain in peaceful retirement, embellish the final resting place of her son and pray for the repose of his soul. And it was there in 1204, at the age of eighty-two, that Eleanor died. She was buried beside her husband Henry and her beloved son Richard. And there you can see her elegant, dignified tomb.

Eleanor of Aquitaine was, without a doubt, the most

charismatic and powerful woman of her age. Accomplished, intelligent and centuries ahead of her time, she married two kings, gave birth to two more and by the time of her death was related through the marriages of her children and grandchildren to almost every royal house in Europe.

The famous troubadour, Bernard de Ventadour, who was reputedly desperately in love with Eleanor, wrote this song for her:

'You have been the first among my joys
And you shall be the last
So long as there is life left in me'

There have been few women in history who have created quite such a stir in the world. Most have been royal, all have been strong and wilful and they must also have possessed an indefinable something that is rarer still. Whatever that intangible element may be, Eleanor had it in gilded carriage-loads.

* * *

La Grande Pendaison De Cremaillere

When you move from one little stone pile to another in rural France, tradition dictates that you should hold a *'Pendaison de Crémaillère'*, which, despite its confusing tongue-numbingly long title, is just a house warming party. The *crémaillère* is the long hook in the chimney on which you hang your stew-pot. Originally there would have been a ceremonial lighting of the virgin fire, inevitably followed by the hanging of a vast pot in preparation for the enormous dinner to which the extended family, neighbours and close friends would doubtless all have been invited. Even now if you have an open fireplace, as we do, it's *de rigeur* to hang a pot in it for the occasion.

Parties of all kinds are the breath of life in France and we knew that, at some time or other, we would be expected to introduce ourselves to the neighbourhood in this traditionally boozy way. So one cool morning in late May, I spent a spidery hour or so rooting around unpacked boxes in the attic, emerging in dusty triumph with a vast jam-making cauldron, inherited from my woolly-bonneted grandmother. We were all set.

The first commodity on our long list, naturally, was the wine. The nearest château to our own modest pile is literally a stroll away over the brow of the hill. Having informed our neighbours that we were finally about to give our Pendaison de Crémaillère, we decided we'd better pay a belated visit to this establishment. Christian and Margarida Lacam inherited the vineyards of Château Carrigou, but built the current château themselves. Of course we're not talking château as in Versâilles or Chenonceau here. This is little more than a large house with a pigeonnier, but it's stone built, with *caves* for the wine and an impressive tower, typical of many of the so-called châteaux of the region. It took them nine years, between caring for the vines, and now it's almost finished.

"Not quite finished," Margarida told me, ruefully, "it'll never be perfectly finished."

All the same, it was quite a feat, and what's more it's not at all unusual. Most of our neighbours built their own houses and if they didn't their forbears did; it's the obvious thing to do here. Stone litters the fields. All the vignerons have land, the house has to be within walking distance of the farmed land, so the obvious thing to do is build a dwelling on the edge of it. They've been doing just that for the last two thousand years or more. (With a few exceptions during violent religious conflicts, when houses tended to huddle together beneath the shelter of an approved church or in the shadow of a dominant château, creating the fortified villages and hamlets that make this countryside so picturesque.)

Nowadays it naturally helps if you know the *maire* and it helps even more if you happen to have planning permission, but I've yet to meet a *paysan* who feels that's a really serious consideration. Throw it up anyway; the commune will come round in time, seems to be the general rule.

"Would we perhaps like a tour of the establishment?" Christian bared his teeth at us and wandered off without waiting for a reply. I glanced at the beloved. We were demonstrably unsuitably attired for an inspection of the estate. He was dressed in typical Englishman-abroad style khaki shorts and sandals and I was wearing a long cotton dress. But as Christian disappeared behind a vast run of assorted poultry, followed by his noisy pack of even more assorted terriers, we realised there was really no help for it. We dutifully admired and inspected a long stone wall, newly built, four feet thick and about two hundred feet long. He proudly pointed out the perfect proportions of the front. Straight as a die, beautifully finished. "Now look at the back," he ordered, hauling me up to get a better look. I watched in interest as the upper part of my cleavage embraced a pair of startled firebug beetles, snorted some stone dust out of my nose and bent my mind to the issue in hand. The wall was all over the place, loose rocks, bends and curves and bits missing.

"Pas nécessaire!" Christian grinned, lowering me to decorous safety and shifting his Gauloise to a more comfortable position at the same time. The other side ran along a public footpath and why bother to spend time and effort on the side that nobody but hunters and ramblers would see? That was unanswerable, so I didn't attempt it and spent the time in a more gainful manner, trying to brush the stone dust from my dress. Glancing down the length of the perfect wall I wondered what he'd built it for anyway. The poultry perhaps, but surely it was a bit of a marathon for just a few hens and the odd guinea fowl? Of course the true reason was obvious and logical. It had been built with leftover stone from the house building, and to keep said ramblers out of the vineyard.

The curs milled round our feet, snapping and jumping up and down playfully. They came in all shapes, sizes and temperaments but seemed to have one characteristic in common. They were all monochrome. The beloved asked how many there were exactly, it wasn't easy to count, and apparently we weren't the only ones who found it a bit tricky.

"Je ne sais pas!" Christian grinned.

A short tour of the closest vineyard was suggested.

"*Desolé!* But we have a dinner engagement at eight o'clock," lied the beloved, improvising at a turbo-charged rate, "perhaps we could come back some other evening, we really just popped up for some wine, forty or fifty litres should do it."

"Beh oui, le vin?" Christian looked a teensy bit surprised, as if he'd forgotten all about it. Had we got a container? Well no, actually we hadn't, we did mention that if he remembered? Hadn't he got one?

"Beh oui, c'est possible," he looked about him in a somewhat distracted manner and lifted his hat for some head scratching inspiration. He'd just pop down to the farmhouse. The beloved looked at me, his eyeballs making frustrated contact with his fringe. The farmhouse in question was the original *domaine* building, as old as the hills and inhabited by M. Lacam senior. It was theoretically only next door, but in deepest rural France next door can be half a kilometre away, and in this case it was.

After another thirty of forty minutes of talking in a stilted and brain-numbing manner with Margarida about neighbours, wine, the price of bread and the prospects of another hot summer, Christian re-appeared with the required apparatus; wonderful! Now could we just fill it up and go? No we couldn't. First we must have an aperitif, a ratafia perhaps? Maybe we would like to try a Fenelon? A delicious mixture of cassis, *apéritif aux noix* and Cahors wine, Christian explained. Then he poured four glasses without waiting for a response.

This powerful local concoction is named after another local luminary; a fifteenth century bishop who became almoner to the sun king, Louis XIV. He spent his formative years at Cahors University and consequently has an aperitif and a street or two named after him. We seated ourselves on nearby barrels, courteously dusted by Christian, sipped our drinks and resumed conversation.

Two and a half hours after we'd popped up to our neighbours' house for the party wine we were finally permitted to leave, totally exhausted but triumphant. In the back of the car we had fifty litres of good, 2003 AOC Cahors. Two euros a litre. Bargain.

*

To say that I was nervous would be to wildly understate the case. I had sixty or so guests expecting a damn good party, with gallons of wine and massive quantities of local delicacies. The wine was in the bag, the food I could cope with – just – it was the non-English speaking contingent of the partying business that was getting my knickers in a serious knot. It's all very well inviting dozens of people you don't know terribly well to a party, if you share their language, culture and social background. Quite another matter if you have none of those lubricating essentials to ease the wheels of conversation.

By six o'clock on the appointed day my hyperactive senses had been partly lulled by several glasses of wine and partly reassured by the sturdy presence of two of my cousins. They just happen to have a holiday home in the Charente and had endured a five-hour drive to join in the fun and lend a hand – though I hadn't mentioned the lending a hand bit on the invitation!

By seven-thirty the effects of the wine were wearing off and serious nerves were beginning to set in again. The first knock almost sent me into orbit. The guests arrived in a huge rush and a torrent of dialect French. Flowers, pot plants, bottles of homemade ratafia (nearly all ratafia is homemade), Champagne, vintage Cahors wine and ancient cheeses were all pressed on me along with a flurry of kisses and greetings.

Another bang on the door and a gentleman with a drooping roll-up in one side of his mouth, a bottle in one hand and a dog collar in the other, emerged with an ominous rustle from the dark shade of the buddleia.

"B'soir!" he mouthed with difficulty, pressing the bottle into my arms and removing his fag to kiss me. He waved it over the hound hanging patiently from its collar.

"Boulette!" He introduced her with casual insouciance, and disappeared into the mêleé followed by the afore-mentioned canine guest. Actually we were well acquainted with the mutt in question; she was the village dog in the little stone hamlet where we have our holiday cottage, and an absolute darling. It was just that this event occurred fairly early on in our new life, we were still a bit British and not very used to entertaining dogs at parties. Pass the canapés and the Pedigree Chum... not that dogs in France would be fed with it anyway. The leftovers of the family casserole and any other scraps are the general diet; they look surprisingly well on it too.

After an hour or two of steady eating and drinking I was beginning to feel a little more mellow, the guests were in full flow and the volume was outrageous. As most were out on the terrace I'd no doubt the whole valley was well aware of the proceedings, and I began to wonder if there was anybody we should have invited and hadn't. Almost certainly. Still, I consoled myself, downing yet another glass of Cahors, you can't get everything right first time. We'd know more people in another year or so and repeat the event annually; from which you can deduce conclusively that I was already pretty well pickled.

"J'aime les pâtés, ma chère", one of my gourmand neighbours complimented me, having helped himself to at least two slices of each of the three whole terrines. He put his fingers to his lips and kissed them reverently, before returning to the table in case I'd hidden anything else behind the vase of oleanders. The main courses were brought in and my indispensable cousins stitched themselves into the kitchen to wash, wipe, mop-up and generally keep the party on track – well more or less on track. Around midnight we served the dessert course. The much-loved local speciality, *tarte aux noix*. It's made all over the Quercy and Perigord in many different guises and there are dozens of different recipes. My favourite is a classic open tart with the walnuts cocooned in a sticky, sumptuous, caramelised filling. It's very filling, horribly fattening and utterly sublime. I have adapted it to suit our tastes and use slightly more modern ingredients, and I find a ten-inch tart will easily feed a dozen people; it's very rich. So with those numbers in mind I'd made three for the party and a selection of other little tarts, along with a whopping chocolate gateau. These I'd assumed would be plenty. I'm not an inexperienced hostess and I'd never seen such a mass of food disappear in one party before; oh yes, it should be plenty. I was making careless assumptions after a large Sunday lunch and forgetting the one salient fact that meant all my careful calculations went for nothing. This is France. They all disappeared with alarming speed.

Out by the pool somebody was carolling 'Lady in red', in a rather wobbly baritone, presumably to his partner. Over by the fireplace Boulette was wolfing the remains of somebody's discarded *pâté de truite fumé*.

"I say old girl", an inebriated friend of my uncle's sidled up to me "You haven't got any more of that nutty pie have you?"

"…is dancing with me…", bellowed the man by the pool.

"I'm awfully sorry Edward," I whimpered, side-stepping a

seven year old in a tutu, "There's a little more *tarte aux citron,* I think"

"That the lemon one? No thanks old thing, I'll have a bit more of that runny cheese instead." He held out his plate and swayed to the music, whilst I tried to deduce exactly which runny cheese he meant. I don't think it would have made much difference, but he was clearly in need of something to mop up his insides.

"I'll cut you some fresh bread." I told him, and sat him down at the kitchen table to sober up.

"Perhaps we ought to open the window?" an indispensable cousin suggested, performing the deed.

"…la, la, la, la", warbled the man by the pool.

Out on the terrace the smoking element of the party, that is to say the French contingent, were getting stuck into the Armagnac and it occurred to me, a trifle tardily, that I'd neglected to provide ashtrays. The tidier guests pressed the flowerpots into service and the gravel on the lower terrace soaked up the rest.

It was past one o'clock and the beloved was beginning to escort some of the elderly neighbours to the front door. A girl in a scarlet shift shot past him, gamely pursued by one of the local councillors. Lady in red? An indispensable cousin poured her an Armagnac and a cup of black coffee.

"I say old thing, like your frock!" Edward woke up in appreciation. "Have a bite of this, not a bad cheese, not bad at all!"

In the hallway the beloved was dishing out coats, whilst in the drawing room the sofas had been pushed back and thoroughly sloshed guests were doing justice to the BeeGees.

"Tragedy!" They yelped in unison, elbowing each other in the ribs, "when the feelin's gone…"

I sank into a chair and gratefully accepted a coffee.

All in all, I think it probably was a damn good party. I can't remember if I ever thanked my indispensable cousins properly for all they did that night, but if I didn't, I do now.

★ ★ ★

A Stroll Through Orchids

The insistent drone of thousands of bees lured me along the rocky track towards the wild service tree. An oddball in the tree world, it's a rare cousin of the rowan that grows on limestone soils and prefers undisturbed primary woodland. Apparently its unattractive brown berries were the grape and grain of northern Europe in medieval times. They were greedily gathered to make the powerful brew known as chequers, a legacy that still lingers on in the many Chequers Inns found in southern England today. I glanced up at the old tree, it was heavy with blossom and the bees were so numerous they hung like amber earrings, ten or more to every quivering head. It looked like a good year and, come autumn, I decided I'd have a crack at the recipe.

A gentle promenade through vineyards and oak forest had seemed like an enjoyable way to spend a beautiful afternoon. The beloved had gone off on business of his own, the children were at school and I was thrown back on my own resources. It was time I started to get my startlingly unfit body into some sort of shape for the summer. Five kilometres winding steeply downhill to Albas and the glorious river would be a pretty good start.

I packed a small bottle of Evian, five tissues and a jumper, closed the front door softly behind me and set off, feeling mightily adventurous.

At first it was delightful. The air was soft and warm, too early for the fierce summer heat and the slight breeze made it a perfect day for a walk in the woods, little clouds scudded across the great arc of sky, as blue as the Mediterranean, and as enticing.

The *chemin rural* that runs up to our house becomes no more than a track after a just few metres, running in a tunnel of sun-dappled green along a terrace of the hill. On the upper side the vineyards of our neighbouring château slope down to the crumbling stone wall, whilst on the lower our own land falls sharply downhill in a tangle of scrub oak and scented shrubs. One day we'll sort it all out, I reflected, there must be enough dead and collapsing wood there to keep Cruella burning for many a winter. It needed managing.

Back on the track I waded on through long blond grasses sprinkled with waving wild flowers and tangled with honeysuckle and dog roses. I was coming to the end of the tunnel and turned sharply downwards towards a little stone house on the main road. Although, theoretically, it is a main road, it's narrow, winding and very steep, so on average I suppose it only sees a car once every ten minutes or so. I stopped to examine the little house. Imagine a long abandoned witch's cottage from the golden storybooks of childhood; it was a bit like that. It was built stoutly of stone, with a large bread oven and a good well. The little garden where she would have grown her herbs was now wildly overgrown and the woods had encroached on all sides, oak, wild cherry and chestnut. Honeysuckle rampaged over the stones, vines grew out of control over the thick wall and a huge yucca bloomed merrily amongst the collapsing foundations on the southern side. It was a beautiful place, enigmatic but a little eerie. I left it to its dreams and continued my ramble.

There were no cars in sight or sound as I reached the little road. It was one-thirty by this time and naturally no sane Frenchman would be out and about. The whole of France was comfortably at lunch, in cool dining rooms behind half-closed shutters, or under large vine-covered terraces on the shady side of the house. 'Mad dogs,' I thought wryly, as I crossed the road and began the climb up to the Croix de Girard. It is a surprisingly steep slope and my shocked knees soon began a campaign of savage complaint. To either side of me wild flowers still bloomed riotously, every few steps revealed another little gem, orchids and cornflowers, poppies and scabious, carpets of thyme and tufts of lavender, valerian and santolina. I breathed in the sights and scents for the first half hour or so, but after that my flabby winter thighs began to scream, my chest heaved unbecomingly and the never-very-good knees soon reached the end of their tether. Fortunately, just as I was contemplating throwing myself down to examine the wildlife at closer quarters and possibly saving myself a heart attack, I emerged at the top of the rise. There, spread out in painterly perfection were the ravishing, long views of the Lot valley. I stood, panting gently, and admired the orderly vineyards and the way they resembled a reluctant boy's still damp and well-combed hair.

Taking a few cautious sips from my water bottle, I put my hand on my heart – just to make sure the damn thing really was still pumping – and carried on. That had been the hardest bit; from then on the ground was almost level, there were swells rather than slopes, great clatters of wings as the odd startled buzzard took off, and scuffling amongst the vines as disturbed partridge gathered their broods and shot out of sight. And every now and then there was a sudden long vista of the Quercy Blanc. It was idyllic.

After another five hundred metres I came to the Croix. It's an ancient wayside cross. Heaven only knows how long it's been there, but the base looks as age-old as the hills on which it stands. The carving on it is strange, even the letters are strange. It isn't French. As I leaned against the pedestal and steamed in a highly unfeminine fashion, I wondered if it could be Latin. But actually it doesn't look much like Latin either, though it's so obscured by lichen it's difficult to tell. Maybe it's Occitan, I mused, the native tongue of this land, which would make more sense. I could just about make out the date, 1600 – or possibly 1660 – but to be perfectly honest I was too knackered at that particular moment to give much scholarly thought to the inscription. Sinking gratefully down to the short grass beneath it, I leaned back against the warm, sun-soaked stone with a profound sense of relief. I was facing due south with the round base at my back. Drawing up my knees, I ruminated on the history of these surprisingly common wayside crosses. They are found in the most out of the way places and, like this one, frequently at a crossroads or junction. A guide for travellers, a compass? Many believe the original crosses were related to weathervanes. Several were adopted by the Christians and are now used as places of roadside worship. But whether it's a guide, a pointer or a shrine it's a sacred spot, a peaceful spot and as good a place as any for a well-earned breather.

Putting my hand out for another liberal dose of Evian, I discovered I'd inadvertently collapsed amongst another cluster of orchids. Wild orchids are a feature of the Quercy landscape; not only are there a great many of them, but a huge variety. This little treasure turned out to be the Pyramidal Orchid. A few paces away there was another gleam of rosy mauve on a tall stem. (When I looked up this splendid bloom in my dusty tomes, I discovered, to my great glee that it was *cephalanthera rubra*, the Red Helleborine.)

A sudden rattle and cough in the distance signalled the end of the lunch break, and a few minutes later a farmer crawled into view on his rusty old vine tractor. He parked twenty metres or so from the cross and unloaded himself, foursquare and pleasantly full. He nodded at me and set about the business of spraying, whilst I heaved myself to my feet and set about the business of walking.

The Croix was the high point of my walk; from there, I mused, it should be all downhill and not too hard – even for me. The sloping sides of neighbouring hills, densely forested, reminded me that there were wild animals out there. Deer of course, by the thousand, buzzards and kites, hare and rabbits, foxes, squirrels and countless other small rodents, but also wild boar. A lot of wild boar, and at this time of year they would be nervous. They were said to be extremely shy, but a nervous, shy boar could still cause me untold damage. I put the orchids carefully in my capacious jacket pocket and firmly picked up a stick.

The zigzagging route that winds through the immaculately groomed vineyards of Château Eugenie, down to Albas itself is a delightful stroll. The vegetation is slightly exotic, leafy and wild, and I bounced down the path feeling light, happy and at one with nature – until I heard the growl. It was a low, menacing rumble, the sort of noise nobody wants to hear whilst alone in the woods. There are no bears in mainland France now, although the brown bear was once common all over Europe. So, if it wasn't a bear, what the hell could it be? I stood frozen to the spot; my ears swivelling like radar, stick held out in front like a stave. What if there were one or two surviving beasts in these wild oak forests? There were thousands of acres of unexplored woodland for them to choose from. They could still be here; how did these desk-bound naturalists know for sure there were no longer bears in France? I knew there was a small colony in the Pyrenees, protected and supposedly well-watched, but after all the Pyrenees were only a couple of hundred kilometres away as the crow flies, and as the bear runs. Or perhaps they could have migrated from the frozen wastes of Russia – let's face it who wouldn't, given the chance? It was all entirely possible. It was more than possible, it was probable.

My fevered imagination ran on. What would a hungry bear do if he'd been travelling for weeks, had just found a nice place to settle and a tasty little morsel just happened to cross his path? He would eat it of course!

I tiptoed cautiously down the path, not daring to run, every sense in my body on red alert. Suddenly the quiet forest seemed full of noises; odd, unidentifiable noises. I took a swig of Evian – just to prove to myself that everything was perfectly all right and I wasn't really scared – and crept on. It couldn't be boar I reasoned, boar don't exactly growl and this was a loud, low and definite growl. By this time I had almost reached the outlying farms of Albas and I was beginning to feel just a mite better. I rounded a clump of prickly yucca – a magnificent sight with countless six-foot blossom spikes. I stopped to admire them, congratulating myself on my calm handling of a potentially dangerous situation. Behind me came a sharp crackle of leaves. There wasn't a sigh of wind and I halted dead in my tracks.

Out of the undergrowth slunk a long, lanky, loping apparition. It was a hound, probably a lost hunting dog, of doubtful genealogy and almost certainly the cause of my unprecedented fright.

"You dreadful *chien*," I addressed the hapless mutt. "You scared the socks off me!"

He wagged ingratiatingly and rolled his eyes, then by way of amendment, turned and prepared to accompany me down into the village. We halted at the village cross for a rest and a drink, and then crossed the main square to the *boulangerie* for something a little more substantial. I sat in the sun at the foot of the memorial and he sat at my feet in a shaggy, spotty heap. We shared a warm, crusty *baguette de compagne*, spread with homemade *pâté de forestière*. It was outrageously messy, but I didn't care and my adopted hound was scrupulously tidy. Not a crumb remained.

We held our impromptu picnic in the Place de la Dime, where three of the four village fêtes are celebrated. Four parties a year sounds a little over the top for a village of this diminutive size – they have a special committee to organise them too – but Albas is nothing if not ambitious, it always has been. In days gone by when the river ran red with wine, the lifeblood of the region, this little village was the great warehouse, a buzzing and thriving little port. Not any more, the Lot is no longer fully navigable and the millions of bottles of Cahors wine produced each year no longer travel the world by water. Nevertheless the ancient vineyards are still here, the dark, luscious wine is still made and drunk here, and the vast labyrinths of caves hidden under the houses are still there. I crossed the main road – one car a minute – and wandered down the dark cobbled Rue de la Carrière to the riverside. All the houses in this narrow thoroughfare have huge arched doors at the base, proclaiming the existence of the ancient caves beneath.Valerian grows at the edge of the cobbles and vast tangles of ivy and vines hang down from the stone facades. My new friend tagged along, snarling at competition, growling at innocent village cats that peered nervously from behind overflowing pots of scarlet geraniums, and liberally anointing an abandoned tractor in the tiny Place Bonamie.

At the bottom of the street the view widens to take in the great panorama of the valley and you find yourself right on the river, opposite the Bar D'Esplanade. I turned to admire the most breathtaking sight in this part of the river valley.

The Albas cliffs are stunning, almost sheer and crowned with a lush, green circlet of unlikely vegetation, the ancient mairie and the equally ancient church. I stood for quite a few minutes just drinking it all in, but the insistent aroma of coffee wafting from the bar beckoned. I needed a more thirst quenching drink. Plumping down in one of the outside chairs, I ordered a *grand crème*, addressed the mutt with a stern accent, consulted my watch and prepared to wait for International Rescue in the form of the beloved and an ancient Volkswagen. It brought a little problem acutely to the fore. I glanced down at the snoring heap at my feet and wriggled uncomfortably. Actually he was quite a big, shaggy and distinctly odorous problem. It was entirely possible that he wouldn't be admitted to the interior of the rescue vehicle.

Abandoned hunting dogs are a perennial headache round these parts, especially at this time of year. When spring arrives elderly dogs, or dogs that perhaps don't quite earn their keep or won't last another season, are frequently dumped in the woods to save the cost of feeding them over the summer. Some, of course, are genuinely lost and will either find their way home again, or will be collected by their owners. Those are the lucky ones, the ones with a collar and an ear tattoo. My snoring, spotty, malodorous friend had neither of these valuable assets and had obviously been living as a vagrant for some considerable time. His best hope was an introduction to one of the charitable souls who round up these dubious characters, take them home, clean them up and have them innoculated, tattooed and otherwise made socially acceptable. The next step in the rehabilitation process is to advertise for a new owner, after which advice is liberally dispensed and the dog is happily relocated. They are a sort of Battersea Dogs' Homes en France. The one we know best is called Poorpaws and is run by Sue, a charming, highly energetic and desperately over-worked part-time waitress, who spends most of her spare time and money caring for these hapless hounds. I resolved to phone her as soon as I got home.

Having finished my coffee and nudged the current cause of my anxiety into life, I wandered down to the river itself. The Place des Gabarbiers isn't really a square at all; it is, as the name of the bar opposite suggests, the esplanade. Only part of it is level, just enough for a satisfactory game of boules, then it runs quite steeply down to the old stone quay. Two hundred years ago wine barrels would have rolled up and down this wide, sloping quayside. I could almost hear the heaving and straining, the shouts and the laughter. I glanced down at the abandoned slipway. Only fisherman and tourists use it now, but in its day it was the throbbing heart of the village. Spotty helped himself to a drink from the river with much slurping and splashing, and I picked a few spring flowers from among the overgrown stones and almost trod in yet another glorious clump of orchids.

Half an hour later found us sitting at the end of the single-track bridge that makes its way from the village on the south bank to the Château du Port and the walnut groves on the north. In the distance a distinctive grey blur gradually materialised.

"Thunderbird One," I murmured to my companion, and prepared to go into battle on his behalf.

"What," asked the beloved, with good reason, "do you call that?"

Spotty rolled his eyes and wiggled his hind end ingratiatingly, while I hastened to explain the circumstances.

"Just let me get this crystal clear," went on the heartless one, "he frightened you almost to death and now you want to take him home and feed him?" I agreed that it sounded a little bizarre, but that was the general idea.

"Then I'll ring Sue," I promised, "she'll know exactly what to do with him."

"I can think of several things to do with him right now," muttered the beloved obscurely. But he shuffled the umpteen supermarket bags about in the boot and ushered my malodorous friend aboard.

By the time we'd driven 500 metres we had all the windows open. Spotty, it seemed, was not so much in need of a bath as a steam clean.

Back home on our terrace we attempted a deodorisation process before introducing our adopted mutt to our extremely overworked friend, in the vain hope that it might make him a little more appealing.

"Grab his hind end will you!" My hero's frustration was mounting as he tried to manipulate both the hose and the unwilling recipient of his attentions. I complied to the best of my somewhat feeble ability. Spotty retaliated by shaking himself like a hearthrug, watering the geraniums, the lemon trees and me. I'm not at all sure who was wetter at the end of it all. We tied the newly clean hound to a stout beam on the terrace, gave him a bowl of water, the remains of a ham hock that had been intended for tomorrow's lentils and the loan of an old towel, whilst we went in urgent search of our heroine.

Twenty minutes later an almighty barking, spitting and caterwauling signalled the arrival of Tinia. This may be our house, but in canine terms she considers it very much her territory, and this shaggy, soggy intruder had no right to be there. The beloved hung on to Spotty, whilst I forcibly removed several rolls of highly aggrieved Labrador.

Later that day a neighbour dropped in for a handful of olives and a few glasses of pastis, and recognised our interloper at a glance.

"Mais c'est magnifique!" He'd been missing for nearly two weeks we were told – and we could well believe it – the owner was a friend of his, he had several dogs, but he was particularly fond of this one.

"Why isn't he tattooed?" I asked, "and why hasn't he got a collar?"

Bernard explained that many farm dogs are not tattooed. You have to pay for it after all! He was more puzzled about the collar.

"Maybe he ate it?" The beloved suggested sarcastically. Bernard nodded and held out his glass out for a refill.

"Peut être."

Our kindly neighbour swayed off, with Spotty in tow, and less than two hours later we received a phone call from the grateful owner. He turned up next morning, straight from the market, with a huge bouquet of purple artichokes and a beribboned potted plant as a thank you. It was an orchid.

★ ★ ★

Stone Walling

Now that the social essentials of our move to this little community had been temporarily satisfied, the house was in some sort of order and summer was in full swing, we decided it was high time we turned our attention to the garden. More accurately to the bones of the garden, the stone walls.

Dry-stone-walling is a glorious and lasting form of building that one finds all over Europe wherever the stuff is plentiful. From the hills and dales of North Yorkshire to the mountains of Calabria and the distant sierras of Andalucia. In the Quercy there's so much of it that it's used for virtually everything – even the kitchen sink!

Firstly there are the terraces; retaining dry-stone-walls, essential if one is to farm these dry, scrubby slopes, many of them now sadly neglected and collapsing into reproachful piles. Most are probably Roman in origin, built for the long lines of famous vines that once lubricated the throats of long-dead emperors and, since the phylloxera disaster, lie deserted and overgrown with scrub. It may be, now that Cahors wine is regaining a foothold on the international markets and people are beginning to realise what an unheralded treasure lies hidden here, more vines will be planted and the terraces will be resurrected. I can only hope so.

Secondly there are the dividing walls. These are more like the walls you find in North Yorkshire. The land is scattered with the ubiquitous white stones, so in order to plough efficiently they have to come out, and once out they make perfect barriers, preventing your neighbour's sheep getting in and decimating the crop. They are far more durable than fencing, and absolutely free, which makes them highly desirable in the eyes of rural Frenchmen.

Thirdly there are the medieval bastide walls. Hugely thick, high and imposing, built to protect villages churches and châteaux against marauding hordes and still surprisingly common. Even the tiniest hamlet is quite likely to sport a thick bastide wall around it.

Lastly there are the much less necessary boundary walls. Some are truly ancient, running along almost forgotten property lines and now collapsed into little mounds, drawing waving blond grass and juniper over their heads.

There are two or three terraces in our own garden, in a shameful state of collapse and totally overgrown with scrub oak and Mediterranean pine. There hardly seem to be enough of them for the land to have been used for vines, but maybe much of the evidence was swept away when the house was built. Either way, they were far too big a project to tackle at that point. A more pressing problem was the swimming pool enclosure. When we moved in an outstandingly grotty wire fence, neither beautiful nor practical, had encircled it. It came out immediately and I tentatively designed a wall around the pool area. It was to include olive trees, one of the four symbols that mean warm southern France to me. It should be a fairly rough and ready wall, we decided; built with the rough and ready stone we'd acquired at Crayssac, and surrounded by masses of gravel from the local quarry at Villesèque. We hadn't quite got round to visiting the gravel quarries, so the wall came first.

Therefore, when the beloved's brother, Tim, rashly announced his intent to pay us a long-overdue visit, he was more than a little startled to find that he would be required to spend half his weekend working as a mason's apprentice. Naturally France Meteo was forecasting the hottest weekend of the year so far. I felt a little apprehensive about the proposed enforced labour and wondered aloud whether a local mason may not be a better option. The beloved was utterly scandalised, and fortunately, so was his brother.

This is a common problem in our household. Maybe it's because I was born and bred in the comparatively wealthy southeast of England that my concepts and visions tend to be on a larger, more lavish scale than those of my nearest and dearest, whose true northern thrift occasionally has to keep me in severe check.

"I think," Tim announced at breakfast, a week later, as he gazed at my slightly coffee-splashed plan for the pool area. He paused and looked round for support. The beloved was scanning the cloudless blue above. "I really think it's a bit too elaborate, I can't see why you need so much of it anyway," (northern thrift again) "wouldn't it be much shorter and neater if you brought it in closer to the pool?"

"Well yes, it would of course, but it wouldn't be as beautiful and it wouldn't frame the view quite so well."

Tim adjusted his aviator sunglasses and addressed himself to the coffee.

"Besides, that olive tree would be on the wrong side", I pointed out. He gave his brother a suppose-we'd-better-humour-her glance and squared his shoulders.

"I'll make you a paella for dinner", I promised ingratiatingly, knowing the market in Cahors would be stuffed with the raw ingredients that morning. Knowing too, that absolutely everyone hankers after paella when on holiday, especially in these parts. We're close enough to the Spanish border for this fabulous dish to be a regular sight on the food stalls in local markets. During the season vast pans, a metre or more in diameter, protrude with glistening mussels and pink prawns, simmering, hissing and exuding tantalising aromas. They're always sold out by noon. I would be making my own, especially for Tim. Unfortunately, this well-meaning gesture turned out to be a bit of a *faux pas*.

After a long day of labour in the thirty-five degree heat, we were all more than ready for a little rest, relaxation and a delicious repast. Dinner was served on the warm west-facing terrace with the setting sun in the background, and the potted lemon trees providing a heady fragrance to the evening air. After several glasses of the usual we were all feeling delightfully convivial. Bring on the showpiece. Paella isn't at all difficult to knock up of course, but somehow it always manages to make an impression. The classic Valencian version of glowing saffron rice topped with steaming mussels and a few large crustaceans, just exudes summer. However, although his wife adores shellfish, Tim, I discovered to my absolute horror, halfway through the first langoustine, regards it with deep suspicion.

"More clangers than a soup dragon", muttered the beloved mysteriously, and departed to refill the carafe.

"He'll be all right, don't worry about it," Helen assured me, calmly peeling a prawn the size of a small banana and handing it to her husband. Tim eyed the beast balefully, obviously not quite in tune with his better half on this particular subject. He took a manful bite and pretended to be transported, but I could read the dogged determination in his eyes. Helen continued to peel prawns both for herself and her hapless mate, making a neat little pile of the remains on the edge of her plate.

This is an ability I greatly admire in people who are quite obviously a lot tidier than I am. When I eat paella my plate is littered with debris; mussels cling tenaciously to my napkin, or anything else that happens to be handy, even my sleeve. Prawn shells end up all over the place, as if mass migration has taken place during the meal, and as for the giant langoustines, they're half on the plate, half off, looking for all the world as if they're making a last ditch attempt for freedom. Tim, meanwhile, was making definitely-had-enough noises. He was handed a napkin and a meaningful look. I decided that it might be more diplomatic to attend to my own dinner at this crucial point in the proceedings, and sincerely hoped that my brother-in-law was fond of cheese.

Next morning the enticing aroma of freshly made coffee lured my sister-in-law from her bed, and it transpired that, contrary to grave expectations, Tim had survived the night. He even managed to force down a croissant and several cups of coffee for breakfast and was pronounced fit and more than ready for action.

In blistering sunshine we gathered outside the pool, clutching various assorted gardening gloves and ready for the final push. Tim was firmly in charge, Helen assumed the role of mason's apprentice and the beloved mixed the rough and ready concrete. Even the children were pressed into service, sifting sand that we'd found in an abandoned and filthy pile at the edge of our neglected woodland. I, on the other hand, was very soon dismissed to the kitchen as a totally incompetent and utterly expendable member of the team.

I spent my time happily engaged with vast tomatoes, pools of olive oil and new salad leaves, nipping down to the village for a couple of country loaves from the boulangerie and some good charcuterie from the tiny epicerie over the road – no more fish.

As I sliced tomatoes and tore basil, I could hear a great deal of noise – and the odd curse – from the pool area. Little messengers ran to and fro keeping me up to speed with latest developments, and the number and severity of squashed fingers. The plasters were running out and I'd soon be reduced to strips of old cotton. At one-thirty I finally coaxed them away for a lunch break, at the same moment hearing the slight cough, vroom and rattle of my neighbour's little van as he prepared to go back to work. Lunch at one-thirty? Working in the heat of the day? And of course he would know what we'd been up to; the normal peace of the midday meal had been shattered by the concrete mixer. I was relieved that he couldn't see me; perhaps I'd have time to think up some highly implausible excuse before he came home.

Out on the terrace the workers were relaxing in the shade and congratulating one another on the successful outcome of the morning's labour. The wall was almost complete; it wasn't very level, but did that matter? They eyed me nervously as I tottered out with a vast dish of Salade Quercynoise, a delectable local speciality consisting of duck gizzards – tastes much better than it reads – sliced smoked duck and foie gras, with various green salad leaves and walnuts, liberally doused in an unctuous walnut oil dressing. Of course it didn't matter! I set the plate down. The whole idea was to give the place a more rustic feel and help the pool area to blend in a little more. Well they'd certainly achieved that! There was a round of backslapping and they sat back, noses glowing like beacons, beaming with the satisfaction of a job well done and the pleasant anticipation of a hearty fish-less lunch.

*

The result of over-buying at the stone quarries had left us with a bit of a dilemma and three vast metre-square pallets of stone, parked heavily, centrally and increasingly permanently on the gravel drive. They weren't adding much to the aesthetics of the place and I was determined to do something about it before the beloved got too used to the idea of a permanent rockery. Should we build the swimming pool wall higher? No, I couldn't bear the thought of the concrete mixer, and anyway I liked it as it was, it was primitive, it looked authentic – actually it looked Roman – and it was quite high enough. Besides, I had another plan.

"We could think about building a proper dry stone wall along the lower terrace," I suggested warily one morning, and received exactly the reaction I was expecting.

"What on earth for?" The beloved exploded, scattering flakes of croissant all over the terrace.

I had prepared this argument with great care. It would take diplomacy, determination and a good deal of what the man about the house terms my 'Jack Russell' tactics – I keep nipping at his heels until he gives in out of sheer exhaustion. But in this case I felt I had justice and the angels on my side.

The lower terrace is the garden level on the west side of the house. The side that overlooks the valley and from which our large, overgrown garden tumbles down the hillside. Because it's effectively at the back of the house nothing had been done about making the beautifully straight sweep, immediately butting onto the lower floor, into a usable gravelled surface. Like everything else it was overgrown and neglected. The terrace itself is about a hundred feet long, though only about fifteen feet wide, then it tumbles down to the next level. What it needed was a low retaining wall.

With both of us toiling away like Irish navvies, we built a straight little wall, three stones high and the whole length of the terrace. The beloved went for his shower that evening with his hair half grey and standing on end as if he'd just received a vicious electric shock. I finally collapsed into the bath at half past nine, covered in stone-dust, grime and sweat, and emerged looking like a newly boiled ham. Monsieur the Elder would have despaired of us.

Part two of the reform-the-lower-terrace plan was delayed to allow the beloved to recover his equilibrium, marshal his strength and catch up on one or two vital coffer-filling activities. Once these were at least partly over, we took a trip to the gravel quarries of Villesèque; a mere ten minutes drive away, to see if we could order some of the required commodity.

This little quarry is right on the roadside, so when they're actively quarrying or grinding the stuff up, the road, the trees and most of the surrounding countryside is liberally sprayed with a fine white dust. For a couple of days – or until it rains – it all looks a bit like Santa's grotto.

Cliff walls rear up on all sides, streaked white, grey and pale gold, with large machines standing around looking like prehistoric birds.

We drove into the quarry itself; there was no obvious car park and no obvious office. A small all-purpose Portakabin hung precariously several feet above the gravel layers below, and that seemed to be the obvious and only place to go. The beloved waded through ankle deep grit to be greeted by a cheerful, bouncy little man in a dusty overall. We'd rather expected to be told this was a commercial operation, didn't deliver to private customers, certainly wouldn't think of delivering such a paltry amount as we might require… But we were wrong on all counts. They sell to anyone, lorry-loads at a time of course, but one lorry-load doesn't actually go very far at all, as we were soon to discover.

The question of colour arose. Would we like the darker grey

or perhaps the more golden gravel? Presumably we wouldn't want the white one? Wouldn't we? I hadn't realised I had a choice in the matter, but when I came to think about it, I supposed gravel would come in different colours as well as different grades. I asked why we wouldn't want the paler one?

"Sun glare Madame!" He said, looking at me as if I was three-quarters stupid. "Nobody wants any more white Quercy stone than they've already got do they?"

I shifted my position slightly, and admitted that actually I rather liked it, the more intense light the better. He thought I was crackers, naturally.

Two days later the order arrived. A sturdy tip-up truck chugged up our unmade drive and arrived at the entrance where our present-from-Crayssac had been proudly installed and carefully engraved with the sort of tool a dentist uses on your teeth. (I felt it too!) The driver checked that he'd got the right house and asked where we wanted the stuff deposited. We explained the logistics of the problem. The gravel was intended for the lower terrace. There was no made-up drive to it; it was just passable for a four-wheel drive car but armpit-sweatingly-steep and not really to be attempted with a lorry. Besides, the angles… the new swimming pool wall…

These ludicrous objections were swept aside and our valiant driver leapt back into the truck, readjusted his roll-up, stuck his head out of the window and reversed round the house, past the swimming pool and down what I had considered to be an impassable slope, at breakneck speed. I scuttled back inside before I was forced to witness something too unbearable to contemplate.

Down on the lower terrace the beloved, the driver and the tip-up-truck were conducting a highly professional sledging; dredging and shovelling performance that wouldn't have disgraced the snow ploughs of Gstaad. In just twenty minutes the whole terrace was covered with a flat white surface – from which there was indeed a good bit of refraction, but I wasn't complaining – there wasn't quite enough to go round the corner, it didn't quite stretch as far as the pigeonnier and there was nowhere near enough to do the hitherto-impassably-steep bit, but that was okay; another day. The hero of the hour wound up his window, shot back up the slope – narrowly missing the septic tank – swerved round the pool wall, signed himself out with a few carved ruts by the lavender hedge and hurtled back down the drive with a cheery wave of the hand. Some performance!

We wandered back to inspect our gleaming new terrace, it certainly was very pristine, and perhaps it was a little dazzling. Still, it would soon get grubby; I consoled myself, then it would blend perfectly with the rest of the stone, which after all must be the same stuff. Arming myself with a few handfuls of basil and a big bunch of parsley from the huge herb pots, I wound my way back up to the kitchen, leaving the beloved to gloat over the gravel and rearrange a shovelful here and there.

I soothed my exacerbated nerves by constructing an altogether more peaceful spread on the upper terrace. A delectable tomato salad dressed with walnut oil and lemon juice, pungent *aillet*, black olives and basil formed the centrepiece. A long, warm loaf of crusty bread with the remains of yesterday's wild boar *pâté*, and a soothing bottle of Clos Triguedina's best, filled the gaps. Somehow I felt we both rather needed it.

★ ★ ★

Scarlet Cherries and Green Walnuts

Beautiful, bountiful June, when the loveliest fruit of all takes its bow. The glorious cherry has everything going for it, an abundance of fruit early in the season, a colour to brighten the dullest day and a flavour to transport you. In England cherries have been thoroughly beaten back by the rampant popularity of soft fruits like strawberries, raspberries and blueberries. I can't understand why. Raspberries, I'm prepared to admit, may have a case. They're flavourful, still seasonal and can be quite delicious, but the ubiquitous, watery, buy-it-all-year-round strawberry leaves me cold.

Now consider the merits of the cherry, the wonderful, aromatic, richly glowing cherry, a fruit fit for a princess. Even the name, here in France, is enough to make the taste buds tingle in heady anticipation. *Une cerise.* The little scarlet fruits quickly ripening in the mid-summer sun are an absolute delight. It's a treat to wander down to the bottom of the garden during the balmy evening, swinging your raffia basket and picking just enough for dessert and perhaps a few more for breakfast. Of course if you've got a big tree – or several big trees – you can make preserves as well. There is no better accompaniment to a flaky, buttery croissant than a spoonful of cherry preserve, except coffee of course, but that goes without saying.

At this time of year the markets are literally rolling in little scarlet orbs. The man-with-a-van, who sells a few live chickens and rabbits and six-dozen eggs, also has a basket of cherries. So does the little old lady who sells the freshest lettuces and a few bunches of whatever herbs happen to be in season. The big fruiterers and verdurers are snowed under with them; prices drop to rock bottom and still they can't sell them all. Every restaurant adds cherries to the *carte*, every café has *clafoutis* on the *menu du jour*; it's a glorious bonanza. Then, as suddenly as it began, it's all over for another year. The weatherman turns the heat up to sub-tropical and the remaining cherries on the trees dry and drop. Within a week the local fruit has changed size and colour, from marble to golf-ball and from *cerise* to apricot.

It is also at about this time of year, when the sun's at its zenith and Glastonbury is contemplating a musical mud bath; when every myth, legend, fairy-queen and demi-god from Scotland to the tip of Sicily is brewing midsummer magic that there is a little magic you can brew up yourself. In France it's called *Apéritif aux Noix* and in Italy, *Nocino*. It's a walnut liqueur, a green walnut liqueur. Traditionally you make it on the twenty-fifth of June, having picked your walnuts the previous evening. Midsummer's day. The reason for such a precise date isn't just whimsy – well there may be a teensy bit of whimsy – the walnuts must be picked before the hard shells begin to form within their soft green skins. As soon as there's any hint of a shell – which you test by pricking with a pin – it's too late, and it happens remarkably fast. I picked two lots, one on the twenty-sixth of June, which I didn't think was bad timing, and one around the tenth of July. The second lot was no good at all. You don't need very many of these nuts, which is fortunate, because they have to be plucked from the trees, not just gathered, and as they're unripe fruits the trees are none too willing to release them.

I picked mine from the vast, spreading walnut on the edge of the hamlet between the country road and a lush green vineyard. Overhead the buzzards wheeled in the thermals, the sky was a shimmering cloudless blue and I was hot. One branch was just within my grasp; I made an ungainly leap, tugged furiously and came away with a handful of leaves and little else. A more scientific approach was required. Taking a gentle hold of the outermost leaves I pulled very carefully, almost holding my breath, and inched my fingers slowly up the twigs to the first nut, a sharp pull and I had one. It was a long, sticky, sweaty business, and I found myself wishing fervently – not for the first time – that I'd been endowed with a few extra inches.

For a litre of delicious aperitif you need about ten nuts. You also need about 700ml of the purest alcohol you can lay your hands on. In these parts that tends to be eau-de-vie, but it could just as easily be grappa or vodka. You need a good bit of sugar and some nice fresh spices. Spices are a highly individual choice. Most of these recipes depend heavily on the traditional four; cinnamon, cloves, nutmeg or mace, with perhaps some ginger. I find the inclusion of ginger too heavy, and cloves too overpowering, so I leave them out. In the end I plumped for a pretty safe bet, a broken stick of cinnamon, a little mace and a long, curly strip of lemon peel. The cinnamon I had in stock, lemons grow in exuberant abundance on the terrace, but mace required a trip to the market, where the spice stalls are spread in tantalising glory. Over a hundred spices, dried herbs, fragrant rosebuds and goodness knows what else spill over the edges of a twenty-foot display. I find it irresistible and have to exercise enormous restraint. After all, 200 grams of one particular spice will last a very long time and I'm a bit of a drip when it comes to asking for very small amounts of a commodity usually sold to restaurants and other commercial establishments in much larger quantities. So it was that I approached with due caution that morning and, having identified the mace – of which I needed only enough to fill a teaspoon – I thought it best to stock up on some of my more commonly used spices. He's a kind boy, the gangly youth who serves on this stall, and would doubtless forgive the eccentricity. My packages piled up and I asked for my mace.

"Petit peu?" I asked apologetically. He dumped a shovelful into the scales and glanced at me eyebrows raised. Oh dear. I tried to explain the minute amount I required. He reduced and reduced the mound in the scale until the weight was so indistinguishable he gave up on the scales altogether, sprinkled it into a bag with his fingers and threw it in as a job lot.

"Merci bien," I smiled as I packed my little parcels round the enormous bouquet of asparagus that had snared me on the way in. He nodded and moved on to the next customer whilst I trundled off in triumph.

This expression of gratitude, we gradually discovered, is one of those common errors made by the average Englishman when visiting France. We're not an effusive race on the whole, we wouldn't dream of greeting our neighbours French-style, or bidding good day, *bon appétit* or *bonne soirée* to a total stranger. We do, however, make sure we've said a very thorough thank you to everyone, from the girl at the checkout to great aunt Mabel, who sent a knitted scarf last Christmas. At school, most of us were taught that *'merci beaucoup'* is the correct phrase to use for all occasions. It isn't. This gushing expression of gratitude will immediately mark you out as a foreigner – if it hasn't been guessed already – and unversed in local etiquette. As a general rule, a simple *'merci'* is sufficient thanks. If you wish to be more expansive the expression to use is *'merci bien'*. *'Merci beaucoup'* is reserved for much more effusive occasions and means 'thank you so very much, terribly grateful, you're welcome to come to my house, drink my wine and help yourself to my walnut harvest, any time'. Which is perhaps a little over the top for an exchange at the cheese counter.

Anyway, back to the shady terrace of my favourite café, where I decided to sojourn for a quick *Perrier menthe*.

I laid out the morning's haul on Florian's rickety table and wondered about my *Apéritif aux Noix*. Despite my stallholder's cautious pinch with the mace, there was still too much for a litre. I should either make two litres now, I decided, or make one now, see if it looked promising, then make another in a couple of weeks or so. No doubt all this stuff about picking on midsummer's day was just myth and folklore anyway. Which, as you will have surmised, is how I came to pick my second, totally useless batch of nuts.

I arrived back in the kitchen raring to go. The temperatures outside had turned themselves up to Sahara and it was a tremendous relief to step into the cool, dim kitchen and pad barefoot on cold tiles whilst I collated all necessary ingredients for the great experiment. The ten nuts were laid out carefully on the chopping board; they had to be quartered with the utmost caution, walnuts stain anything they touch. I recall reading somewhere that British colonialists fleeing from the Indian uprisings of the nineteenth century, stained themselves with walnut juice in an attempt to pass as natives. Some of them presumably achieved it and survived to tell the tale. It's strong stuff. I sharpened my knife and hopped about a bit wondering where to make the first incision. They're surprisingly hard and the first one shot off the board and across the tiles, with me in hot pursuit. Honestly, as if I wasn't hot enough. I took a firmer grip on the reluctant fruit and delivered a blow that very nearly gave me a manicure as well. After a fairly fraught five minutes I achieved the required forty segments and deposited them into a litre decanter. It was a plain glass style with a wide top, the sort you find on a million café tables all over France. I added four tablespoons of sugar, which is another highly individual choice. You can add up to six or seven ounces if you like your aperitif sweet, or none at all if you're a fan of the very bitter. Green walnuts are extremely bitter, so I prefer to add a little sugar. The spices went in next and then a splash of the fragrant white wine my neighbour had pressed on me the previous day. I hadn't the faintest idea what it was; the bottle was unlabelled, as his home-consumption wines always are. Then there was the eau-de-vie that another neighbour, with a still, as well as vines at his disposal, had donated. I carefully topped up the litre carafe and sealed it with a handy piece of Clingfilm. It's supposed to sit in the light for six weeks, whilst it gradually changes colour from clear to a soupy green – alarmingly like an old fish-pond – to a rich brown. Then you filter it at least once and store it in a dark cupboard until Christmas at the very earliest. I placed it reverently beside the open window and kept glancing at it all day. Christmas seemed light years away.

★

Early one afternoon, a week or so after my midsummer madness with eau-de-vie and mace – when any sensible person would be either digesting a huge lunch or taking a quick siesta – I found myself in searing sun, once more stirring my pots.

I was on painting duty. It had been decided that the shutters at our holiday cottage, Le Pigeonnier, were now scruffy, grotty and in need of immediate resuscitation. A crooked election had been held and yours truly scandalously voted the best qualified to administer the kiss of life to the ancient *volets*. Appeal was pointless; I gathered up my son and heir and trundled off to the nearest Interbrico for a pot of that indefinable bluish colour the French like to use on their shutters. In the north it tends to be greyish, the further south you go the more blue it seems to become, unless of course the shutters haven't been painted for thirty or forty years (surprisingly common), by which time the Mediterranean sun has obliterated the original hue anyway. There were dozens of different blues to choose from, in numerous different forms, gloss, satin, matt and so on, inside, outside, wood, plastic, bathrooms, kitchens… the list was endless. I plumped for one of the most expensive, all-purpose, one-coat, dry-in-thirty-minutes varieties in *bleu lavande*, a colour I felt might possibly complement the dozens of struggling young lavenders under the windows, and proudly bore it home. Now, truth to say, I've never really been much of a one for extensive preparation when it comes to painting anything. Slap it on – carefully of course – and hope for the best has generally been my motto, which in part explains the events that followed.

I set up my rickety garden table, laid out my brushes, eyed the accumulated, and in some cases inhabited, cobwebs balefully and washed them off quickly with the kitchen mop – five foot handle you see – and that was it. I was halfway through the first shutter when I was hailed vociferously from above. I looked up to see the young man who'd been painting my neighbours' shutters and staining their wooden terrace, on and off for the past week.

"B'jour Madame," he started well at any rate, but the conversation rapidly deteriorated after that. I wouldn't have understood much of it in English, let alone dialect French.

"What sort of paper are you using?" He bawled, from his precarious perch on the balustrade.

"Pardon?" I enquired, dimly.

"You know!" He grinned and made vigorous up and down motions with his clasped hand. The square was deserted. My son had wandered off in pursuit of his own essential activities, and I was effectively alone.

"Ah", I twigged belatedly, relief flooding over me. Sandpaper! "Yes, I've got a sanding block," I told him, in my stilted Parisian accent, holding it up in triumph.

"Non, non! C'est un papier universel. Merde!" He was getting a little heated for some reason, and came bounding down the *bolet* to explain my shortcomings to me. After a five minute discussion on the merits of a good, rough bit of paper – something I've happily managed to avoid all my life – he fetched some from the boot of his car, gave me a cursory nod and took himself back up to continue with his own business. I checked that he wasn't looking, gave the kitchen window a quick run over with the good-rough-stuff then levered open my paint pot.

I love the thick, glossy, hopeful quality of a new pot of paint, and I was quite happily giving it a thorough stir and admiring the swirls of mauve and indigo disappear into a glorious, shimmering pale lavender blue, when I was hailed once more from the oracle above.

"Have you got a product for the twenty-four hours?"

"Pardon?"

"The twenty-four hours! You know, the insects and all that. Which product are you using?"

My French may be a little limited, but to be fair he could have been trying to communicate in either Oxford English or Mandarin Chinese and I wouldn't have been any the wiser.

"What sort of product, exactly?" I enquired. He discoursed

at length and in monosyllabic French – as if explaining to an incredibly thick four-year old – on the need to prime the windows, and especially the shutters, with some sort of preservative to prevent my house being munched away by insects. *Capricornes* especially were rife around these parts, was I aware of this? Of course I wasn't.

So, I must have a product. He had an example in the boot of his car, though it actually belonged to my neighbour, Xavier, who'd presumably already paid for it. It was an insecticide, fungicide and all round magic stuff. I must have some and I must use it on everything, everything! It would take twenty-four hours to dry and then I could finally paint my windows blue. He gave me the rest of Xavier's tin and stumped off.

Damn, damn, damn! Now I had two lots of painting to do.

★

Francine stared at me in shocked amazement. "You don't preserve *haricots verts*?" We were standing in the bowels of her larder whilst she instructed me in the elusive art of Quercy home economy. I tried to explain that I really preferred my beans fresh, I wasn't overly enamoured of the grey-green shadows that emerged from those numerous kilner jars in mid-winter, but Francine was unimpressed. Naturally fresh beans would be better, but they cost an absolute fortune out of season. She'd seen them for five euros a kilo in February, and – even worse in Francine's eyes – they come from Morocco! Unfortunately that cuts little ice with a woman who's paid £1.99 in an English supermarket for a bare handful of Kenyan grown beans.

"Well you will like some now of course." I certainly would. Francine, like other ladies of the region, has a vast, delightful and very productive potager and at this time of year the insignificant little *haricot* features heavily, the staple food of the south and eaten daily.

"Have you got your potatoes for the year?" Francine changed tack. I hedged and pointed out that we don't have a *cave* like hers. A veritable treasure trove of preserves from *pâtés*, *rillettes* and various parts of the duck, to tomatoes, beans and strings of onions and garlic. The potatoes were stacked in old sacks in one corner, the drying *haricots blancs* in string sacks in another. There was a large tub of salt and another of black peppercorns, then came row upon row of confitures and *compotes*, numberless jars in jewel-like colours preserving all the luscious richness of summer. The third corner was devoted to the original purpose of the *cave* and the life-blood of this particular family; wine. As Francine's in-laws happen to be local vignerons, wine in their house flows more freely than water. Consumption is limited by taste, will power or loss of consciousness. The final corner was occupied by a large stand that in the winter months held the lemon tree. I wouldn't have thought it possible to keep a tree in the dark like this for so much of the year, but Francine explained that she opened the double doors as much as possible during the day and the tree survived quite well. It certainly did; it must be a good eight feet high and provides her with enough lemons for the whole year.

"So," she returned to the attack, "have you got your potatoes? Your *cave* is quite big enough for that, oh and I've got some melons and tomatoes for you. You'll have to deal with the tomatoes today or tomorrow of course, they're very ripe." She hauled out a large wooden box from under a pile of old sacks. I watched in some trepidation, in case there were some unknown squatters who could possibly outrun me, whilst Francine piled the box with umpteen kilos of huge, misshapen and ever so slightly squashy tomatoes.

"Really, Francine, thanks awfully" I whined – I was way out of my depth here – "but I honestly don't think we can eat all these..."

She waved my pathetic demonstrations away.

"Of course you can't eat them all now. You need to bottle all those long ones – she meant the ovoid, Italian variety – have you got plenty of jars?"

I explained I had a fair stock of pretty jam jars that I used for chutneys, pickles, fig compote and the odd few kilos of cherry preserve.

"Oh, and for mincemeat at Christmas."

"For what?" She stood up, abandoning her ferreting among the tomatoes, and stared at me in amazement, "You don't put raw meat in a preserving jar?"

Oh dear.

"No, of course we don't actually put raw meat in jars. Well they did in days gone by, and some still do, even now, but not for very long or it would go off."

"Of course it would go off, you can't preserve meat that way!"

I did my level best to explain the provenance of mincemeat. I even gave her a rundown of the ingredients I use in my own recipe, but she remained utterly unconvinced, and not to be deflected from the main issue.

"So you need to go to the Interbrico or the Catena to buy some good jars. They aren't very cheap, but of course you only have to buy them once, and there you are, tomatoes for ever."

I could allow her the pith of her argument here. If tomatoes are cheap, or better still, free, then perhaps one should consider such a method. But we use a fair few tinned tomatoes in the winter months, I'd need an awful lot of jars, and, as Francine admitted, they weren't cheap. I reckoned I'd need about a hundred at about a euro each. Even if I paid nothing for the tomatoes I used, tinned toms are so cheap anyway it would be about three years before I saved any money at all, and so much work. No, I definitely wasn't convinced.

Meanwhile Francine had moved on to garlic. There was another bone of contention here. I had a couple of strings hanging in my kitchen. Of course garlic won't keep that way, it needs to be stored in a cool dark place. I was well aware of this; my lovely long plaits were merely decoration. I was also well aware that Francine wasn't likely to view such an arrangement with much approval. Nor did she.

"What do you mean decoration, you don't eat them at all?"

"Well, no." I tried to explain that in England hanging strings of garlic and peppers, chillies and dried herbs were very avant-garde at the moment. You want them on display, not just in your cellar.

"But they'll dry out. They won't keep that way." Francine persisted; " If you want strings of garlic in your kitchen" she gave me a speaking glance that told me, in no uncertain terms, that she couldn't understand why anyone would, "you can buy artificial ones from the garden centres."

"Ah, but they're even more expensive than the real thing aren't they?" I countered, sidestepping a large arachnid and beginning to flap around like a hyperventilating hen.

"They are, yes," Francine admitted, calmly putting a terracotta pot over the offending beast, "but you can't eat them can you? They aren't food and they will last forever." I gave a mental bow to her earthy wisdom. That last little phrase defined the rural Frenchman's whole philosophy of life; 'They aren't food.' Food is not wasted here, nothing is wasted. If you buy a goose you use every part of it from head to foot, the same goes for vegetables. To buy a whole string of garlic and then not eat it but waste it, so nobody else can eat it either, must seem like sacrilege. Meanwhile Francine was scrabbling in another large container.

"Here have some of these melons, I've got far too many." So saying, she pushed the tomatoes to one side of their rickety box and loaded it with seven or eight yellow-green cannonballs.

Her generosity was embarrassing; I would never be able to reciprocate.

★ ★ ★

The Season of the Fêtes

By the beginning of July 2006, Europe was in the grip of World Cup Fever. On the Saturday of the quarter-finals our daughter's school held its annual *kermesse* – summer fête – attendance was obligatory and in any case this was her swansong, she was going on to the *collège* in September. The afternoon was much like all such affairs; little games to make a bit of money for the school, refreshments and a lot of standing around while the children chattered to various friends and posed to others. The evening was to be a different matter altogether; a proper, full-blown, four-course dinner. It was held in the magnificent village square. In this case it was also interspersed with much leaping up and down and a great deal of shouting, *"Allez les bleus"* from the gentlemen present. They had even hauled a television from a nearby house to facilitate viewing. France were playing the legendary Brazil and would be lucky to win, all support was necessary. More than that, it was a patriotic duty and any man seen not to be bellowing encouragement at the top of his lungs would have his access to the pastis – in other words his life support system – cut off.

Meanwhile, we had another party to attend, and raced off to it, arriving late and staying just long enough to thrust a birthday gift at our startled host, down one quick drink and hold a twenty-minute chat about the state of the forest, before haring back to Castelfranc for the dinner. It was supposed to start at seven-thirty but it wouldn't of course; such things never start on time. We finally made it well after eight-thirty. The barbecue had just been lit and the men folk were happily gathered round the television, thoroughly tucked into the pastis and waiting for the kick off. Couscous and salad finally arrived – to my express relief – at nine fifteen. The meat didn't make its appearance till after ten – by which time Zidane had the men of the village completely hypnotised – and the cheese had to wait until after the final whistle.

Against all expectations, France won. Church bells rang, the *mairie's* flags waved in the warm breeze and children danced in triumph. When some sort of self-control had reasserted itself on the ecstatic inhabitants they turned their attention back to the table and polished off all the cheese, the two metre square *tarte aux pommes* and the rest of the barbecue for good measure. Celebrations make you hungry!

*

"Amanda!" A voice hailed from on high. I poked my head out of the kitchen door.

"Stéphane!" My neighbour smiled and came haring down the *bolet*, two steps at a time.

"I want a jug."

"Do you indeed?" I went out into the place to meet him.

We were back in Le Pigeonnier for the season along with

half a dozen other summer residents – our bachelor neighbours included – which can be highly entertaining. Of course they tend to keep holiday hours, around midday to about four in the morning, except on the night of a fête when they'll generally make an effort to stay up until well after dawn. It means mealtimes are exceedingly erratic, they and their floating population of friends tend to emerge, blinking in the harsh light, just before the shops close for lunch. Somebody will shoot out of the house, wearing nothing but a pair of baggy shorts – if we're lucky – and a tousled hairstyle, leap into a much-dented car, race like a demon to the nearest *boulangerie* and return laden with baguettes or croissants. After that little burst of activity, things tend to slow down for the siesta, they come back to life again in late afternoon, down to the river for a swim or a vigorous game of table tennis in the *place* – which can get surprisingly competitive – boules or even football. In the late evening somebody will be detailed for the galley or barbecue. The latter is a heap of large stones behind the collapsing old village wall. Water is carried to the site of the industry in an ancient bucket to save bothering the *pompiers* in the event of an emergency. Remarkably responsible I've always thought. Tonight it was obviously Stéphane's turn.

"What sort of jug?" I glanced back at the fat terracotta example on our terrace. It was overflowing with sprigs of bay from the tree that grew at the base of the old wall, and a vast bunch of parsley handed to me by a market trader that morning. It somehow didn't seem quite their thing.

"A litre, you know? For cooking."

The penny dropped, a Pyrex jug. I hauled one out from the depths of my old dresser. It still didn't really seem their thing.

"What d'you want it for?" I asked. He looked at me as if I were as thick as a small Citroen, sideways on.

"We want some mashed potatoes of course!" And with a

boyish grin he turned on his heel. Now I was really puzzled. How the hell could he use a jug to mash potatoes, did he crush them with it? Ridiculous. Maybe it was to measure the milk and butter? But that seemed almost as daft. I was more than a little intrigued. He kept me in suspense for twenty-four hours, and inadvertently revealed the secret the following evening. The beloved had nipped over for a pastis and came back nursing the object in question.

"You know why he wanted it?" He was well aware that I'd been pondering the riddle on and off all day. I shook my head and waited to be enlightened. He stuck his arms out by his sides and walked stiff-legged towards me. Then to my intense amusement assumed a ludicrous, wide smile and chortled like an out of control Martian... Smash!

We may be in the gastronomic heart of France, a place where the best fruit and most glorious vegetables are as abundant as the wine, but a bachelor pad is a bachelor pad, the world over.

*

That evening we took ourselves off to our cosy local auberge. The ever-smiling waitress, dressed in her habitual outfit of t-shirt and leggings, showed us to our usual table and went to fetch water and the breadbasket. She returned to tell us the various *plats du jour* and the beloved's eyes lit up. Steak Tartare is an all time summer favourite of his, which he'll always order when it's available. I plumped for the *gigot* of local lamb, raised on the high plains of the *causses* and succulently roasted with a flageolet bean puree. *Un grand* of the house wine, a good local Cahors from the vineyards behind the restaurant, completed our selection. We sipped a little wine and waited for the noisy party of our fellow countrymen, at the long table in the centre of the room to settle down, before trying to exercise some sort of restraint at the sumptuous buffet. Our two children had no such compunction. This little hostelry is their favourite restaurant, and they returned with plates laden with various local *saucissons*, salted anchovies and numerous salads, not to mention rather larger than necessary slices of the huge *terrine de campagne*. I reassured myself that lunch had been a small and fleeting affair. They would undoubtedly be hungry.

I spent a few enjoyable minutes pottering round the display in a fog of indecision before selecting a piece of the enormous poached Salmon, a delight. Meanwhile the beloved had little trouble with his own vast slice of *terrine*, so little trouble that he went back for a second course of various other delicacies.

First rule of French dining; never go back for a second helping.

It was at this point that our enjoyment was interrupted by a furious commotion at our neighbour's table. Their main course had arrived, and it was clearly not quite what they had been expecting.

"How can we eat that? It hasn't been cooked!" Barked a red-faced turnip with a ginger moustache.

"You should send that back, love!" The over-loud moans came thick and fast. "Don't you worry, I'm going to, damn thing's completely raw!"

"The other girl told us this was a steak with tartare sauce on top!"

Our poor, flustered waitress tried to explain in her desperately limited English, that that couldn't possibly be the case, but her voice was drowned in a cacophony of complaints. We flushed with embarrassment at the ridiculous scene, apparently so common in rural France that many more commercial establishments will routinely ask any English person if he is aware that the Steak Tartare he has just ordered is a raw dish. Fortunately, this little *auberge* happens to have a waitress who is either a Frenchwoman, brought up in England, or the other way round. I suspect the latter; she speaks English perfectly and with the clipped accent of the Home Counties. Equally, her French is flawless, so flawless, that until that day we'd no idea she had any command of English at all. She has always addressed us in French, and we rather assumed she was yet another of the extended family that runs this little *auberge.*

Within a few minutes she had calmed the rowdy group, and told them they could have their Steak Tartare cooked, like a *Steak Haché.* I returned to the exquisite puree accompanying my lamb and thought privately that it was rather more than they deserved. After all, even if they had been a little puzzled by the dish they had so confidently ordered, they surely didn't need to be quite so impolite.

By the time we had finished the delicate, pink lamb and the beloved's Steak Tartare – raw and delicious – we were, as usual, getting a little over-full. Our waitress was trying to tempt us with a *'belle tarte aux poires'* that she assured us was just out of the oven. I could smell the delicious, buttery, caramelly aromas drifting from the kitchen and would dearly liked to have tried it, but it was no good. The temptations of the huge buffet and a good breadbasket on an empty stomach had hijacked dessert yet again.

Second rule of French dining; no matter how warm and delicious, be parsimonious with the bread.

I settled for a *cabecou,* a small disk of the pungent local goat's cheese, whilst the beloved and the children dithered over a selection of *glaces.* For some inexplicable and slightly weird reason, the beloved is unusually fond of a 'Smarties' ice cream, a choice that causes great hilarity amongst the staff. I finished with a quick shot of coffee, something I find almost impossible to forgo after any meal in this civilised land. Whilst my son loped through to the bar to collect the bill, I surveyed the ancient stone walls of the restaurant, converted from a thirteenth century mini-château. My eyes were drawn for the umpteenth time, to the swords worn by our host's grandfather and an ancient photograph from the early days of the twentieth century. This is still a family business, and they're proud of their genealogy.

The bill arrived in due course; fifty-eight euros. It rarely exceeds sixty for all four of us, which is incredible, but not at all uncommon in the little auberges of rural France.

As we left I thanked our host for the splendid dinner and felt like apologising – though I'm not entirely sure why – on behalf of our English neighbours. A Chad-like wail followed us into the night.

"What, no Stilton?"

The smiling waitress lifted her hands and gave an imperceptible shrug.

It's the season, they're used to it.

*

Every city, town, village and hamlet in France, of whatever size, has its annual party. Some have two or three, Albas has four, Cahors has several more, and of course Paris is non-stop party. But if there is only one it will be in high summer, so that everybody, from the smallest child to Madame Dubois – who reached her centenary last year – can attend. Days before the event over-wide businesslike lorries start to arrive to put up lights or decorations, or both, perhaps there'll be a fairground ride for the children, perhaps a marquee for seating.

In Rouffiac we dispense with all this and take pot luck on both the weather and the children's behaviour. Food is supplied by the participants, luscious *tartes* and quiches, huge bowls of salad, dripping with dressing, vast home-made pizzas, stuffed peppers and tomatoes, couscous and rice, speckled with freshly chopped herbs. The tables and benches are borrowed from the *mairie*, the bread is made in an ancient bread-oven on the edge of the hamlet and the wine comes from the local vineyards. Both bread and wine – absolute staples – are covered by the price of the ticket. Even entertainment is somewhat random, but as everybody is pretty well intimately acquainted with – if not actually related to – every other soul in the village, there's no shortage of good conversation. And as long as there's an abundance of wine, warm breezes and starlight we're more than happy to go with the flow.

A large village fête is an entirely different cauldron of onions, and one of the most boisterous and popular in the valley is organised by the *mairie* in our sister village. In rural France it has become impossible to maintain a *mairie* in every little village and hamlet, so only the larger villages have one and the surrounding hamlets, some no more than three or four dwellings, are taken under their wing. Sometimes there are two villages of almost equal size, so to prevent bad feeling the names are tacked together. For instance, a few kilometres away we have Anglars-Juillac. The church is in Anglars, the *mairie* and the primary school are in Juillac and everybody's happy except the postman.

Our little hamlet is in the same boat, the *mairie* is in the other village, so are most of the facilities, and the fête is correspondingly larger and better equipped. No bringing along a homemade *tarte* or a bowl of salad to this one, it's a full-blown five-course meal, places limited to roughly five hundred. Tickets must be bought in advance – or at least the day before – and it's wise to mark your pitch. This last is a peculiarity we'd never come across before, and were initiated by our neighbour, Xavier, who raced across on the afternoon of the fête to stake his claim.

The tables were laid out in the *salles des fêtes* where the band would be playing, and in a large and highly convenient barn nearby. This isn't always the case; if the weather is indisputably dry, the tables will be laid outside. But on that particular day the air was incredibly hot and sultry, even for the Quercy, and there'd been the odd rumble of thunder. The prudent members of the *committee des fêtes* were taking no chances.

Xavier chose the barn as the more suitable of the two locations, and proceeded to mark our required twenty-two places at one of the long tables. It's not a matter of elegant place names. You take a pen, draw a line on the paper tablecloth at either end of the chosen area and scrawl your name in the middle, Rouffiac x 22.

Back in our hamlet the cats were lying in the baking dust of the *place* as we squealed round the corner and finally came to a screaming halt in the dead grass. Boulette opened one eye and closed it again, flopping back down into the cool shade of the lilac trees. It was going to be a hot night – in more ways than one.

"How do I look?" It was seven-thirty and we were making lethargic preparations for a mass departure. Stéphane stood in front of our stone steps, brows lifted, arms extended. "Sexy?"

"Girl bait!" I assured him, pulling my tummy in and wondering whether my newish jeans would stand the colossal strain of a five-course dinner. At least I looked reasonably presentable to begin with, I decided, wondering if my outrageous flattery would merit a compliment in return.

"Good." He raked his hair back into place and went to take his place in the convoy. I shrugged, obviously not.

The village of Carnac was bursting at the seams. There were cars parked everywhere, at impossible angles, in impossible places. The road through the centre was totally impassable. We arrived with high-speed panache, and the beloved – thoroughly and alarmingly integrated into French driving techniques – nudged the old Passat into a ditch and left her to her own devices.

At the impromptu bar, three temporary waitresses were besieged. Bottles of pastis fell like soldiers on the Somme; barrels of wine drained like a bath with the plug out, and when not actually drinking everybody was busy kissing everybody else. I was jammed between old Claude, who was telling me about his trek to Santiago de Compostella, and Xavier, who was nose to nose with a chestnut-haired beauty. Quite an accomplishment, I mused, taking a second out to steal a closer look, since he's a basketball player and a good six foot six tall. When I talk to him my nose is on a level with his elbows. This latest candidate, I noticed, was wearing four-inch heels to enable her to accomplish the afore-mentioned trick. Still pretty impressive though, I'd need stilts.

Dinner was served about two hours later – by which time we were all happily and thoroughly pickled. First came the soup. French Onion of course, but the summer version, which uses tomatoes in addition to the classic beef stock. It was served in the large plastic washing-up bowls always used on these ceremonial occasions and was absolutely out of this world – mind you, I was pretty hungry by that time. This was followed by a traditional *salade Quercynoise* and that old fête standby *confit de canard*. Out of the corner of my eye I could see Monsieur the Elder squeezing past the bench and bearing straight down on me – and any other kissable female in his path – he halted to enjoy himself with Fabienne, who escaped after a quick *salut*, but I was pretty well trapped and undoubtedly in for it.

"Eh ma petite, une bonne fête?" He kissed me four times and stood back to admire the scratches he'd made on my ears, stroking his ultra-smart party beret. He was off to the boules

tournament, he told me, perhaps he'd have a little cheese later and a little more wine, but he wasn't going to dance, too old for that sort of thing now. He eyed me speculatively. Was I going to dance? Oh God. To dance or not to dance? I decided to demur. Claude caught my eye and nodded approvingly. The old *roué*!

By the time the cheeses were served, the party was completely out of hand. At least a dozen live wires, with even livelier hair, were standing on the tables singing raucous songs – reluctantly translated for me by Hélène's son who was visiting for the occasion – and the tablecloths were covered in wine and scribblings. The men in our party had borrowed my pen to draw themselves a grid. Each grid had twelve squares, and each time their glasses were refilled they put a cross in one square, unless somebody else was using the pen, in which case they didn't bother. This was done in order to keep a strict tally of the amount of alcohol consumed. Of course the aperitifs didn't count, neither did the vast quantities doubtless consumed in the seven hours between the end of the meal and the departure of the convoy at six-thirty the next morning. But it's necessary to keep a careful eye on these things.

Out in the square children were shooting silly string and party poppers, the girls behind the bar were back in business and the band was pumping out the blues.

"I need you baybeee..." bellowed a large figure propped against the bar, grinning aimlessly at me. "...to warm a loneleee night." He jiggled his eyebrows and burped romantically.

"Darling, I think it's time we went home," I suggested to the beloved, who was nose to nose with old Claude.

"Already?" The latter exclaimed, "It's only two-thirty!" I shrugged. I've got no stamina.

* * *

A Carpet Of Squashed Figs

The last few weeks of summer are lazy. The mercury is boiling in a thousand thermometers and nobody feels inclined to move.

Vignerons prowl slowly round the vines, squinting anxiously at distant clouds; holidaymakers prowl round the little villages, cameras at the ready, squinting curiously through ancient stone doorways and posing in front of the old chapel; the rest of us do as little as possible in the heat of the day, and wait until the cool of the evening to conduct any serious business. Eating, drinking, flirting and partying are the most serious, naturally, but even the more sober pursuits, such as harvesting – the combine-harvesters work all night – and of course shopping, are done in the evening.

I just about manage to summon up the energy to go for a walk round the village each day. The heat bubbles up through my flip-flops and beats relentlessly down on my straw hat, stepping into the shade is a blessed, blessed relief, and one of the most delicious forms of shade is a fig tree. There are a great number of them in these parts, some are wild and quite small and some are a bit exotic and bear very large fruit early in the season. But the great majority are large, wonderfully sprawling trees bearing the middle-sized plum-purple fruit we've come to associate with the name; and in late summer they are laden. The voluptuous scent is almost overpowering, hot, heady and sticky-sweet. It's accompanied by a symphony of wasps, which fortunately have absolutely no interest in humans; they're obsessed with the dew of sugary syrup on the over-ripe fruit, gorging themselves until they can barely fly. When the wasps have finished with it, the fig will fall, dark purple and squashy, and the ground below will be stained that colour. If the tree happens to be on a roadside, there will be a carpet of squashed figs, and if the road happens to be on a slope it'll be very slippery and very precarious indeed. One of the trees on my walk is in just that sort of location; it's also particularly bountiful. Ripe figs freshly picked, with a trickle of lavender honey and a nice dollop of Greek yoghurt are the very thing for breakfast on a steaming summer day.

I set out one exquisite morning with a fairly dilapidated rush bowl and a walking stick – very useful for knocking off bloated wasps and bending a just-out-of-reach branch to within grasping distance. The full heat of the day was still to come; the air was soft and warm and it felt marvellous just to be alive. It was mid-August but the village was surprisingly deserted, the only soul I encountered was old Monsieur Robert, at his ease on the venerable stone bench in the shade of the high convent walls. He could see the whole *place* from there, and all the twisty little roads in and out of it.

Ancient streets in tiny villages, lined with old stone houses, are the television of rural France. Children play there in happy little clusters. Teenagers hang out, eyeing up the competition, honing their courting skills and brewing outrageous amounts of surplus testosterone. The old men play their endless games of boules – seniority dictates the location naturally – in the thankful shade of pollarded catalpa or crumbling stone walls. From there they can see it all and keep an eye on the predatory antics of a group of young black-leathered bikers who are plainly after their granddaughters. Each group watches the others, living their own lives and absorbing the lives of every other soul in the community through every quivering sense.

M. Robert had little to see, it was enough to be out in the warmth of the summer's morning. He called out

"'Jour Madame" and heaved himself to his feet.

I went over to receive my due. He attacked my cheeks dutifully then sank gratefully back down to his cool seat. We made some desultory conversation about the heat and the plum crop, and then I excused myself and slipped round the corner of the convent and down the hill.

The tree I had in mind is rooted on the very edge of a garden, and most of the branches spread over the road. By this time on a hot summer morning the tarmac was a shimmering violet, exuding the sweet aroma of baked figs.

I lowered one branch to pick a couple of beautiful, fat, ripe specimens and used my stick to grab the next sprig... And at that precise moment there was an almighty roar from somewhere round the top of the tree. I gasped in fright, slipped on the mat of fruit and for one wild second could be seen dangling from the branch with my walking stick, tracing concentric circles in the fig puree with my feet. As I regained balance – and equilibrium – I realised that it wasn't a panther at all; it was a fighter plane, just visible now in the far distance. The French Air Force is allowed to practice in the Lot valley because of its low population density, and a low-flying visit from a budding Tom Cruise in the quiet of the morning is startling enough to blow yours ears off.

I smoothed down my rumpled cotton dress, picked off a few dry twigs, ejected an inquisitive wasp and glanced anxiously round. I was quite alone; so I picked up my fig basket and strolled nonchalantly back up the hill – nodding to a completely unheeding M. Robert – to a delicious, peaceful breakfast.

★

Glorious August in southwest France lures tourists as a buddleia in full bloom lures butterflies. The heat, the holiday atmosphere that pervades every little town and village, and the outstanding food and wine available at every turn, have all contributed to make this once neglected little rural backwater one of the holiday hotspots of Europe. For decades the overworked masses have swarmed down from the frozen north to the beaches of the Mediterranean, but gradually, very gradually, tourists have worked inland. They've stopped *en route*, made forays into hitherto untented territory, and discovered to their amazement that the beautiful Quercy holds more attractions than they had believed possible. Now, during the two holiday months, the population more than doubles and nowhere is this more obvious than in the markets. They swell in season, to four or five times their winter size, jammed with lithe blondes in skimpy shorts (much appreciated by some of the locals) and enormous bellies in lively shirts.

One radiant Saturday morning we elected to brave the crowded streets of Cahors, in order to sample the delights of the summer market. I wanted some peaches for a conserve, and our own trees were still too small to bear more than half a dozen fruits each. I needed a whole tray, twenty-four, and if you visit this particular market towards noon on a hot Saturday, you can pick one up for about four euros. And naturally after all the stresses and strains of the bustling marketplace we would need a little lunch.

We scuttled across the boulevard and on down to the cathedral square and the heaving marketplace. It was a cacophony of noise. The serious traders, who rely on these markets for their living, bellowed as loudly as their lungs would allow in order to attract tourists to the local delicacies. The vegetable stallholders, who'd sold most of their crisp, fresh produce by now, stood around chatting to each other, whilst the fruit stalls were still busy. Any local will tell you it's better to wait till the end of the market to buy your fruit, especially on a Saturday. No farmer wants to load up crates of perfectly ripe peaches and nectarines only to lug them all the way home to rot. Much better to get what he can for them. I took my usual circuit to suss out the best and cheapest, selected a small stall by the cathedral door, and moved in. The old gentleman who runs this stall knows me quite well, he lives in our village and has seen me at the fêtes – so he tells me.

"Ah Madame, bonjour, une degustation eh?" I smiled and thanked him, but told him, quite firmly, that I only wanted some peaches. He ignored me completely – he is a bit deaf, but not that deaf – and lined up slivers of fabulous white peaches, a slice of juicy melon, a halved Reine-Claude plum and several little slices of a brugnon – a popular local cross between a peach and a plum – that he'd been sharing with his lugubrious dog. The latter wasn't impressed.

"I just want a tray of peaches." I begged. But no doing, these people are masters of their art, they have to be. I was firm in refusing the melons. I still had the last of Francine's bounty to cope with, but I succumbed to a bag of Reine-Claudes. If you've never had one, let me tell you they are the sweetest, lightest and most delightful member of the greengage family, and the countryside round these parts is awash with them. I also reluctantly accepted four rather over-ripe *brugnons* that he balanced expertly on my tray of huge yellow-fleshed peaches.

"And you must have two white ones, as my gift," he added in a low voice, looking at me from under the shade of his beret as if he'd just given me the keys to his Mercedes. I thanked him weakly, poured a handful of change into his purpled hand and staggered, bow-legged across the cobbles to where the beloved was happily ensconced in an argument about the continuing excavation of Roman and pre-Roman ruins in the city centre. I had enough fruit to feed more or less the entire village.

Late that evening I sat leaning against the warm stone walls of Le Pigeonnier. The sun had lost its ferocious afternoon heat and was gilding me with a gentle glow. On the wall were six pots of peach conserve, cooling in the shade and two rather spontaneous-looking *tartes* that I'd made with the rest of the fruit. There had originally been three, but the first had inadvisably been put out on the wall to cool before I'd quite finished the clearing up, and gratefully consumed by the village mutts. Boulette, chief protagonist in the crime, looked up from her slumber amongst the lavender bushes, and gave her lips a thoughtful lick. I stared stonily back and we came to a silent mutual agreement. She yawned, gave herself a thorough scratch and turned over to cool the other side. A dog's life in southern France is pretty good.

All around me the insect life, disturbed by the dog, settled back to business on the low Mediterranean shrubs. In an hour or so Boulette would race off home to supper, as her builder-master pulled into the square in his big white van. I would be going in to bang about with pots and pans, and the children, grubby with the day's play would be going in for a dunk in the bath. But out on the hazy lavenders, the hummingbird hawk moths, butterflies and bees would dance on in an entomological ballet that would last to the final streak of sunset.

★

Of the many delicacies to seduce a visitor to this part of France some of the most famous and most delicious are the *confits*. As a rule this means wonderful duck or goose, salted then cooked and preserved in their own fat. Not necessarily, however. Another very popular variation is *confit de porc*, a delicious alternative to ham which I first ate one warm, late summer evening in a friend's garden. He happens to be an excellent cook, the down to earth sort that calls a spade a spade, a saucepan a saucepan and doesn't disdain the use of a pressure cooker.

We were invited to dine at seven-thirty and turned up at eight, which was just as well because Rob was still working. He and Kim have been here six years and their house is still only half finished; the garden half flowers, half jumble of sand piles, log piles and stone, the old kitchen warm and inviting rather than beautiful. It's not at all House and Garden but it's one of the most comfortable places I know.

We crunched over the previous year's walnuts, dodged the cats, and made our way between the sand piles to the little stone alcove they use as an outside dining room. The sun was just beginning to sink into a pool of molten gold, spreading along the horizon, turning the sky violet, saffron and rose. Kim arrived with the olives and a well-chilled bottle of pink. Rob pulled on a fleece and they both sat down. Dinner was served.

We ate homemade *pâtés* and sausage, more olives and plenty of country bread. The wine, which was made by their next-door neighbour, ran out and was replaced by a substantial Cahors from a little further down the valley. I sat back to take a well-earned breather while Rob brought on the *pièce de resistance*. He served his *confit* in cold slices with a juicy tomato salad. It was delicious, oozing with garlic and surrounded by an aura of bay and thyme. My totally kitchen-blind beloved was enormously impressed. We ate so much of it that we had little appetite for the fresh apricots that Rob had skilfully run under the grill and served warm for dessert. I sat back and sipped my wine.

This was one recipe I had to have and one skill I definitely needed to acquire.

*

"Well bugger me, look at that!"

It was a bare week after our first encounter with a pork *confit*, and the beloved was scanning the menu board outside our regular café in Cahors. I looked at him in some surprise. He's not usually quite so vociferous.

The dish that had caused the outburst was one of the chef's specialities – as opposed to the *plat du jour*, which changes daily – there were only three dishes listed and the last of them was a *confit d'agneau*, their own, home-preserved lamb *confit*. It seemed this practice was even more prevalent than we'd previously supposed.

The beloved flagged down one of the waiters, who swung round, tray balanced dangerously on two fingers, and wrung his hand.

He would save us a table of course, in or out?

I glanced at the gladly sparkling fountain, the cicadas were in full cry and the skies were as blue as the Virgin's robe. I couldn't go inside today.

We skated round the market in double quick time, then I queued for my scrumptious baguettes at a particularly popular *boulangerie*, and was delayed by a tramp who begged so eloquently that I donated one of my golden spears to his cause and had to turn back for another.

Back at the café the lunchtime chaos was at its height. It was twelve-thirty and the entire population of Cahors had poured into the many little bistros and brasseries that make their living in these two short hours. The beloved had seated himself at a little table by some discreetly placed geraniums and was toying with a glass of cool local red.

"B'jour Madame!" Arnaud, another waiter, wrung my hand and pulled my chair out for me. The beloved had thoughtfully placed himself facing the sun. In this café there's a doubly chivalrous significance to this. It meant that I would not only have the sun on my back, I would also be facing my favourite view. Heroic Gambetta and his fountain with the timeworn medieval buildings in the background.

Florian brought me a glass of kir and repeated the *plats du jour.*

"Alors, pasticcio epinards – avec cabecous!" He kissed his fingers and raised his eyes to the plane trees. *Ou poulet roti, pommes sauté et salade."* He switched tongues without warning. "The pasticcio, he is very, very excellent. You like lasagne?" He knew full well I did, so what could I say?

"I'll have the *confit d'agneau*." The beloved stated firmly, before Florian could flog him the *poulet.*

The platters arrived before we'd even finished our drinks. They'd somehow managed to slide the largest portion of lasagne I'd ever seen out of the tin. I sighed and thanked God and the most Rubenesque of his angels that the bikini season was finally over.

The pasticcio was blissful. The salty, tangy goats cheese, set off the vast quantity of spinach perfectly, as for the lasagne, it was perfect, even though there was an acre of it. It was all too delicious to leave. The beloved smacked his lips and savoured his *confit*. It was a shank, beautifully cooked and falling from the bone.

"Les desserts?" Asked Arnaud, shimmying past with an armful of salads. He knew the answer anyway, and collected our

plates on his way back, verifying the size and number of coffees required. We sat back, sipped the egg-cupful of dark liquid – that for some reason I can only drink after lunch and only in France – and soaked up the September sun.

I sipped my coffee, idly watched the pigeons in the huge square, and thought back to the time, just a few weeks previously and in full tourist season, when we'd rushed in here late, about one 'o clock. They'd reshuffled tables and squeezed us into a corner in the cool shade. We had ordered omelettes and salad and a chilled carafe of the house pink. The café was full to bursting, the waiters a monochrome blur, noisy children and impatient businessmen forever on at them. Our lunch was delayed somewhat, not that it mattered a whit. But it mattered to Florian, and when we finally asked for the bill he refused to accept payment. Our waiter brought the money back, and we could see Florian smiling in the doorway, looking to see how we'd taken the news. He gave a little bow. It's a nice place.

⋆

"All set for moving day!" The beloved is never happier than when he is on the move, and we were moving from the cramped, stone confines of Le Pigeonnier back to our more spacious farmhouse that afternoon. The groaning car looked like something out of a Disney cartoon. Unnecessary lengths of coiled rope suddenly appeared behind every seat, the guinea pigs were balanced on top of a pile of old bedding, and I felt in dire need of a large glass of local brew by eleven o'clock in the morning. It's a stressful business.

We finally left the sunny, stone cottages of our delightful hamlet in the baking heat of mid-afternoon. We were loaded to the gunnels, children and spare pillows bursting from every window, guinea pigs staring placidly out of the back, small potted palm poking out of the roped hatch. I would now stay at our calm house in the hills, to unpack, arrange and generally keep some sort of order, whilst the beloved ran the car to and fro like a demented ant, gathering all the miscellaneous rubbish that we'd somehow managed to accumulate during the course of one short summer.

This has become an annual cycle for us now. Renting out a large family house – with pool – in the holiday months, then moving to a little cottage in the heart of a friendly country community, can be a profitable business, and one of the ways we keep ourselves just about in the financial swim.

Down in the cellars I could hear my son chasing about madly, presumably after a small intruder. He reappeared five minutes later holding the culprit by the tail.

"Give us this day our daily mouse," he grinned triumphantly, misquoting to his heart's content, "and forgive those mice that trespass upon us!"

The guilty one eyed me beadily from the palm of his hand.

"Take him up to the barn" I ordered - the usual punishment meted out to the convicted rodents of this particular crime. The barn in question has been disused for years, and stands atop the hill, next to the derelict house where our absent neighbour holds his annual parties. It still seems to hold a fair bit of dry straw, loads of old bits of kindling, small piles of archaic tractor parts and a large, shifting population of assorted small animals. Mousewood Scrubs, without the wardens and with a much better view.

While the sentence was being carried out I took the opportunity to stroll round the grounds, glass of *menthe a l'eau* in hand, to inspect the fruit trees. The figs were bare, the cherries, apricots, peaches and plums had given their all weeks, months before. The two young almonds were struggling bravely with a couple of dozen fruits each. The apples and pears looked promising though, and the persimmon was beginning to show signs of its winter glory, so was the pomegranate, whilst out on the terrace the lemons, limes, clementines and oranges were covered in hard, juicy little fruits. The crowning glory, however, were the olives; small, hard and very green, but olives! The lifeblood of the Mediterranean, I could hardly bear to wait another three months.

A screech and the rattle of gravel in the drive signalled the arrival of the ant from the Pigeonnier.

"Darling! Come here." Bellowed the occupant. I sauntered round to see what he wanted. He grinned bashfully and passed a loaded and very sticky wickerwork bundle through the window.

"Brought you a basket of figs."

* * *

Les Vendanges

Late September and the temperatures were still sizzling. We'd had no rain for weeks and the leaves on my pear trees were drooping disconsolately, like a guilty dog's ears. In the vineyards the farmers frowned, growled and stroked the grapes contemplatively. They were ripe and just about ready for picking but they would have been better for a drink. It has to be supplied by nature too, a vine destined to make AOC Cahors wine cannot be watered artificially. It was too late anyway, having failed to produce a shower at the right time the weather mustn't be allowed to break now and ruin the year's prospects. A good spell of sunshine is absolutely crucial for the harvest and the forecasters were on their mettle; a whole community depended on their getting it right.

The Quercy was holding its breath.

Late one evening we were lingering over a last glass of wine on the terrace, admiring the streaked blood-orange and amethyst of a late summer sunset, when we heard it, that distinctive purr that would trigger pandemonium.

It was a grape harvester; we could just see it in the vineyards belonging to Château Cenac on the far side of the valley. The vendange had begun. Tomorrow they would all be out. The stubby blue harvesters, sailing through the vines like land-locked catamarans, the ancient tractors and trailers, coaxed out of the barns, covered in a fresh veil of cobwebs and staggering round the narrow, serpentine roads dropping little gifts of anonymous provenance and rusty appearance along the way. Children home from school and elderly ladies in their navy print pinnies would be put to work wherever possible. Breakfast would be a shot of caffeine taken standing, lunch – sacred ritual – would be cut from two hours to one, and dinner would be eaten long after sunset. There wasn't a moment to lose.

Next morning, as I bumped down the winding road that twists and turns round the hills to Luzech, I spotted the cavalcade from our neighbours over the hill. Monsieur the Elder was in the lead, followed by a pristine harvester and a tractor that looked as if it was second-hand when Methuselah was alive. They ground slowly to a halt beside me, Monsieur graunched his window down a little further and extended his hand for a greeting – he was too preoccupied for kisses, but to merely wave, or, heaven forbid, ignore me altogether would have been completely alien to his chivalrous French soul.

"Eh ma petite?" He began, predictably. I told him I was *en forme*, and asked him if he thought the weather would hold. He shook his fingers as if they'd just sustained a powerful burn. It's obviously not a question one should ask. Three days would be sufficient, he explained. Of course it's all much faster nowadays; they have the harvesters now. He waved a nut-brown hand towards the peculiar shaped monster behind him; he remembered the days... A prolonged blast on a hooter from a frustrated Renault driver, stuck behind the tractor, recalled him to the present and the urgent job in hand.

"Eh bien petite," he continued hurriedly and almost dislocated his shoulder trying to reach my cheeks.

"A bientôt M'sieur!" My window sighed back into place and I left him to dream of the bad old days.

The land had baked to a deep golden crust in the late summer heat, a haze appeared on the roads, and purple stains began to spread on the hairpin bends where ancient tractors had shed part of the load, doubtless while rushing home for lunch. Elderly machines in the last stages of disintegration were abandoned at the side of the narrow lanes – rusty entrails spewing from their sides – there was no time to waste in nursing, any possible resuscitation would have to wait until after the harvest.

All day long the indefatigable workforces laboured – the colour of our neighbour's skin turned from *crème caramel* to *crème brûlée* in forty-eight hours – even we were pressed into service. In this ancient place where every family is connected with the vines in some capacity or another, every available adult and every reasonably mature child toils until well after dark. And who looks after the younger ones? Any sane adult not directly involved in the *vendanges*, naturally. We qualified on the second two counts – and obviously just scraped by on the first – because we found ourselves running a highly popular, impromptu crèche from sunrise to crépuscule.

Once the grapes were safely gathered and crushed, the skins were hauled off to the old distillery at Castelfranc. Pressure eased and there was time to haul the abandoned tractors out of the hedgerows and coax them quietly into the vast, dark interiors of ancient, owl-infested barns where they'd hibernate until their appointed resurrection the following September. There was also time for everybody to relax and look forward to a storming night out at the *Fête des Vendanges*.

This rumbustious knees-up is a very local event, a cross between a harvest festival and a barn dance, but with rather more oomph and much more sophisticated fare. The new local wine is given its first outing, weeks before the commercial hoo-hah of Beaujolais Nouveau hits the road. It's awful of course, most new wines are, but by the time you actually taste it you will already have eaten a four course dinner, consumed a handful of chestnuts – freshly roasted over the glowing braziers – and drunk two or three bottles of much more palatable local nectar, so your taste-buds won't be on top form anyway.

After dinner, and a dubious *degustation*, comes even more dubious dancing. I am not a dancer. I cannot shimmy my slender hips and wave my arms in a willow-like fashion calculated to drive a man out of his senses. As a child I spent one tortuous night every week for twelve years, in a draughty hall, bending my unwilling legs into frightening shapes in a fruitless attempt to learn ballet, and I can barely manage a demi-plié. This lack of natural talent doesn't seem to matter however. If you have two legs, two arms and enough hair to identify you as female, there's no excuse. The men of these country villages, stoned to the wide, will whirl you across the ancient cobbles until you're unsure whose feet are whose and which arm to grab when you fall. It's exhausting, exhilarating and highly enjoyable.

I bounced back to the bar with my red-faced partner, to where the beloved was quietly consuming a jug of new wine and doing a striking impersonation of Basil Fawlty whenever he was encouraged to dance. I wondered about his ability to steer the car back up the steep, tortuous road to our house. Downing half a glass of Perrier, I took to the floor in the well-upholstered arms of Monsieur Le Comte, a vigneron from the other side of the valley. His style was very much old-fashioned ballroom and, though he didn't mention it, my jigging up and down on his toes could hardly have complemented his smooth-flowing steps. I suspect he may have been trying to waltz, but his spectacular midriff and my woeful ignorance hindered progress a little. We were both exceedingly thankful when the band struck a lively note. He immediately stepped up a gear and bopped around like a Munchkin on Speed, while flinging me from one side of the marquee to the other. By the time I landed back with Basil I was more than ready for a rest, a glass of something fortifying and a handful of newly roasted chestnuts. Huge, hot and more delicious than any chestnut I'd ever tasted in my life, they had the savour of the earth, the fire and early autumn. Naturally I guzzled far too many.

Over by the band I spied our young neighbours, propped up against a tent pole, once more intent on the only other business that would be tolerated in this shrine to the Gods of food and wine. They weren't the only ones naturally; in that little corner of the cobbles Aphrodite definitely held sway.

*

Grapes are not the only harvest. Here in this warm southern land October is not only the month of wine but of walnuts, and the time had just about arrived to gather the latter.

The walnut groves of the Quercy have been around for hundreds of years. Some maintain the original trees were introduced by Eleanor herself – more than likely as she'd travelled widely in the Middle East and yet remained fiercely loyal to her own lands. But one thing is certain, the walnut has naturalised here now. There are hundreds of trees dotted along roadsides, tracks and driveways that provide abundant fare for those quick off the mark, and you do have to be quick; within days they'll all disappear into the carrier bags of waiting peasants, pockets of enterprising schoolchildren and even the car boots of travelling salesmen. They are a tasty and extremely saleable commodity, so if you want a share of this seasonal prize you need to be on the starting line when the whistle blows.

Gathering walnuts is unlike the painfully slow process of chestnut hunting, or the nose-to-the-ground business of mushroom hunting. It's fast, frantic and furious. I have pulled up under a roadside tree, thrown both children out of the car, and pulled away again a few minutes later with six kilos of nuts.

Two over-excited children bounce up and down in the back, sorting their bags and baskets while I screech round to the next tree. We can usually gather as many as we're likely to use in a year within about half an hour. Of course, that's if we get the timing right and somebody else hasn't appropriated the best of the harvest. Another factor to be taken into account in all this munificence is quality. The best nuts are the large, elongated Franquettes. There aren't many of these trees that are truly wild, but quite a few are planted at the edges of vast gardens and plantations where their abundant nuts fall freely onto the road. Fair game.

Last year I loaded my visiting mother into the front seat and whirled her off on the walnut trail. She hadn't had so much fun for years. We stopped under every tree and she'd haul herself carefully out. Basket in hand, neatly skirted bottom in the air, she hoovered up anything remotely nut-like, then staggered back into the car singing "Here we go gathering nuts in May" and re-arranging her petticoats while I drove on to the next appointment. We gathered about fifteen kilos of nuts, and she spent the afternoon happily washing them, fussing over them and spreading them out on the terrace to dry in the sun. It's an immensely satisfying experience.

Once the walnuts were gathered for the year we turned our thoughts to the other free bounty available in the thousands of miles of forest right on our doorstep. Mushrooms, chestnuts and pinecones for kindling. I also had to consider the already ripe fruit from the chequers tree. That first then.

The wild service or chequers tree that grows at the top of

our land is a bit of an arboreal rarity nowadays, but at one time its dull brown berries were much sought after and the basis for the medieval drink of the same name. The name that spawned a hundred pubs – and supposedly the Prime Minister's country retreat – in the chalky soils of southeast England. It would probably be completely undrinkable, but I was keen to have a bash. And first of all I had to gather the requisite amount of fruit. That in itself would be no mean feat. For some reason this rare tree has chosen our garden to establish itself in quantity. We have eleven adult specimens, but the largest by far stands on the very edge of a steep slope, scattered with sharp little rocks. I armed myself with a basket, scissors, ladder and gloves, and sallied forth resolutely set on conquest.

Two hours later I'd picked about two kilos, my hair looked as if I'd emerged from a fight with a combine-harvester, my hands were filthy – I'd discarded the gloves after the first five minutes – every nail was broken, and there were scratches all over my face. I was thrilled with myself. Now all I had to do was turn these unpromising-looking berries into a delightful aperitif. Hmmm. Of course I tasted one of the candidates early in the picking process, and actually it wasn't as bad as I had feared. How can I describe it? A cross between an apple and a lemon perhaps, a crab apple, I think, would be the nearest you could get. It's undoubtedly too sour to eat as it is, but not bitter. I had quite high hopes.

I hung them laboriously over a piece of twine, downstairs in the light and airy cellar – setting up a cacophonous wheek-wheeking from the resident guinea pigs. Hopefully my fruit would blett nicely there and we could get on with the interesting bit.

Meanwhile I had another mission.

*

"I've heard," yelled my uncle down the line, with a fine disregard for the benefits of Mr Bell's most famous invention, "that Château Lamartine 2003 is a damn good vintage. I wonder if you could buy me a bottle or two?"

"Of course," I agreed immediately and extremely unwisely, "how many would you like?"

"Oh about five cases I should think would do it. To go with the *filet de beouf* you know?" I agreed that it would certainly go beautifully with his suggested menu – but five cases?

"For the party of course, about a hundred people, see what you can do anyway," he went on, without pausing for breath, "I'd be very grateful, just the thing, I like a nice rough edge to my wine."

"Good grief. The things I do in the line of duty," I grumbled to the beloved.

My aunt and uncle were celebrating their golden wedding in some style and the onus was now on me to act as official sommelier and not let the side down.

"Rubbish, you enjoy doing this sort of thing." The beloved had no sympathy. "We'll go to the *domaine* for a *dégustation*."

"You know, he said he thinks Cahors has a rough edge to it." I ruminated. It was some hours later and we were digesting our magrets de canard and contemplating an attack on a local blue cheese.

"He meant tannic," the beloved stated imperturbably, swirling the subject of the controversy round in his glass. "It isn't an easy drinking wine after all, it's a wine to be savoured with the richest, deepest flavours," he added – coming over all poetic, "I know exactly what he means."

I took a bite of the firm, chalky blue and a mouthful of our current favourite. God, it was like drinking the elixir of life.

"He's been spoilt, that's the trouble." I muttered to nobody in particular, "Too many bottles of Margaux. If he'd ever drunk the sort of paraffin we used to drink at times…"

"I'm sure he has," the beloved told me firmly, filling up my glass, "which is why he wants a good Cahors."

In the end, our visit to Lamartine had to be postponed for some weeks. Autumn was marching on and the wild harvest must be gathered or lost. It was a cold day in December before we finally got our act together and set out to provide the party with its essential lubrication.

The château, like many in these parts, is just a large stone-built farmhouse, and it was deserted. Low, frowning clouds threatened snow and it wasn't the day to go prowling round ranks of winter-stark vines in search of assistance.

"Now what then?" The beloved asked accusingly as we ground to a halt just inside the gates.

"Well, it says it's open and the gates are open, so I think there must be somebody around." I countered, a little loathe to try getting out and shouting all the same. There was no need. It was open. An elderly individual shuffled in from the vineyards, exchanged his old boots for a pair of decrepit slippers, unlocked the cave, and we were in business.

His son ran the business now of course, he told us conversationally, as he uncorked the first bottle. But he was in the mountains at the moment.

"Le sport!" He made vigorous motions with his arms and nearly took my eye out with his corkscrew.

The beloved enquired about the particular wine we had come to taste.

"Non!" He told us, lifting his beret to scratch his head for inspiration. The entire vintage had been sold to the *négociants*. 2003 was a good year; we'd have a hard time finding it. How about some of this one?

I was aghast. What the hell was I supposed to do now? I had

a wad of euros burning a hole in my pocket and the expectations of a very large family party riding on my shoulders.

The beloved, much calmer than I am in any sort of crisis, turned his attention to the available wines and buried his nose in his glass.

"Try this." He handed me a bare dessertspoonful of sloe-dark liquid. I sipped, and it was fabulous. So was the price.

" Yes, it's wonderful," I agreed, irritably, "but it's far too expensive, and anyway we've *got* to find the 2003. That's what he's expecting."

"There isn't any left, so he'll have to have a different wine, or the 2004 vintage." The beloved told me implacably, picking up the next glass. I felt as if the top of my head was coming off.

"There *must* be some about somewhere, if it's been sold to the *négociants* they will have passed it on. It can't *all* have gone to restaurants."

Close interrogation of our host revealed that there probably was a bit about still, but we'd have to hunt around, much easier to buy pristine new cases from him. Yes, much, I thought dolefully, but it's the wrong stuff.

Eventually we bought a mixed case from the château, for our own consumption, and to add a little variety to the beloved's small cellar. The real business of the day had been a complete washout, and we were faced with a trek up and down the Lot valley to track down the last remaining bottles of the 2003 vintage.

It is unusual for a wine to sell out quite so fast, but there were several contributing factors. Firstly, Lamartine is a small vineyard. Cahors vineyards aren't like the huge fields of the Languedoc or the raked parkland perfection of Bordeaux. They are tiny little patches crammed between encroaching oak forest and fields of sunflowers and lavender, sweetcorn and grain. Secondly, 2003 was not only a good year but a very dry one, so the *vendange* was smaller and there was less of it to begin with. And thirdly, this particular wine had been given the ultimate accolade, a mention in Hachette. It was rare, it was good and it wasn't expensive. No wonder it sold like hot cakes.

We did eventually manage to buy four cases of the required nectar, but only by searching high and low and draining the Lot valley dry.

The party would be held in September, and I had to admit, I was rather looking forward to it.

★ ★ ★

Olives and Lemons

The café/bar in Prayssac is headquarters for the Friday market husbands. While their wives scour the stalls for the finest leeks, haggle over the outrageous price of *salade* or *radis noir* and buy a slightly larger fish with the euro they saved, their poor men-folk prop up the bar, hand round La Dépêche and dispose of a couple of prolonged aperitifs. It's a good place for a morning coffee; especially in summer when you can sit outside and watch *tout le monde*, from the sunny pavement. In winter the arrangement is necessarily a little different.

I blew in with frosted plane leaves at my heels late one Friday morning in early December. The fug was so thick I could barely make out the bar, and the dozen or so regulars were as surprised as they always seem to be at my appearance. More so when I ordered a coffee, it was eleven forty-five, far too late to be drinking coffee, I was asked courteously if I wouldn't rather have a Muscat.

I chose a chipped table, nodded to my neighbours and settled down to enjoy the local rag. The landlord brought me coffee, and twelve pairs of eyes – thirteen if you count the elderly, scabby golden Labrador – followed him. As I showed no sign of doing anything interesting, like removing my top and exposing a bikini – and believe me it does happen –– conversation reluctantly resumed and attention was once more focussed on the level in the glasses.

It isn't easy to understand a man who was born and bred in this part of the world, especially after the age of about eighty, and these characters were all in that category. They've spent their lives smoking harsh tobacco and drinking incautious amounts of some of the strongest, darkest wine in the world. As a consequence their voice-boxes seem to have acquired the same sort of muffled mechanism as loudspeakers at a railway station and the result is a kind of gruff, bellowed growl with a twang at the end, incomprehensible to anyone who hasn't spent a lifetime becoming thoroughly attuned. The two young girls who serve in this bar are decidedly locals and understand every grunt, groan and smoky expletive; they also have hips like *haricot verts* and a liberal hand with the wine bottle. They're a popular pair.

Every ten minutes or so the door will rattle open and another overflowing basket, stuffed with leeks and lettuce, *epinards* and a slice of *potiron*, will be loudly thumped on one of the spare tables. The recipient of the dinner it contains will start to shuffle nervously; he'll drain his drink and turn his collar up and down while glancing surreptitiously at his mate from behind a neighbour. If she shows signs of discarding her coat and accepting an aperitif, he'll clap his friends on the back, light another roll-up and jovially order another glass. This is rare however, she's much more likely to send him a withering look, which hauls him from his place and draws him reluctantly towards the door as if on invisible elastic.

This unlikely pantomime goes on all morning until the last sinner has been forcibly evicted and the church clock chimes the half hour. It is twelve-thirty and time for lunch. Outside in the market, stallholders are packing up, thawing their hands on the occasional brazier and thawing their tonsils with the occasional swig. Inside, the waitresses are bustling from bar to dining room with baskets of bread, carafes of water and bottles of wine. The latter has changed colour. The crisp, pale muscadets and heavy gold Rivesaltes have given way to the pride of the region, and the anonymous bottles now being ferried to impatient diners are the colour of undiluted Ribena.

I discarded my coat and indicated my desire to join them for a typical *déjeuner Quercynois*.

Lunch in this café is a one-menu-for-all affair, and very good it is too. I began with a small plate of shiny, plump violet and black olives, a bowl of cornichons and a slice of nutty, air-dried ham from Bayonne. The bread came from the bakery on the other side of the church; a good chewy, yeasty flute, to be consumed with pace and care. I refused a glass of wine, to the frank amazement of my neighbouring diners. They were all workmen in dusty overalls, cold and hungry, their bellies budging the table to and fro as they reached for the bread or salt. I smiled at the pair at the table beside me and lifted my water glass. They leaned back over their plates in acute embarrassment. These *Anglaise*, honestly, they're just so forward!

My second course arrived, a steaming plateful of *cuisse de dinde confit* and creamy *haricots blancs*, with an aroma to pull a man in off the street. I was informed that my turkey had been simmered in goose fat and garlic, with plenty of herbs, then stored in vats of more goose fat for the last six months. It was utterly delectable, crisply roasted with a melting skin and tender meat just slipping from the bone. My neighbours tucked in with great enthusiasm and wiped their plates clean with bread. I did my best, but I'm really not in the same league.

At the other end of the room a petite lady, slender and chic – and pushing sixty – was wrestling determinedly with her exquisitely permed poodle and downing her third aperitif. A well-heeled, well-wrapped and slightly shifty looking gentleman, thirty years her junior, bustled in to join her. He discarded his overcoat and scarf, communed closely with his mobile and caused the usual restaurant kafuffle. Her son, I thought idly, as I played with my napkin. He kissed her cheeks solicitously, and then went on to ravenously consume her lipstick… Obviously not her son! I made a minute inspection of the crumbs on the tablecloth; it was turning into an entertaining lunch hour.

My cheese arrived, a small disc of Rocamadour from the hills east of Cahors, ripe and runny.

"Tarte aux abricots, glaces ou sorbet citron vert?" My waitress enquired.

I plumped for the sorbet, ordered a *café* to follow and glanced sideways at my workmen friends. They'd emptied their breadbasket with the cheese and were now haggling over the possibility of ice cream as well as *tarte*. Good grief!

After I'd toyed with my sorbet and they had polished off enormous portions of *tarte*, we sat back, sipped our coffees and compared midriffs. (They were feeling much more convivial by this time, and I'm relieved to say that they won hands down!) I left in their company, full to bursting.

At the back of the room the guilty lovers were holding hands across the table, scattering olives far and wide and totally oblivious to the world.

It could only happen in France.

★

"Two hundred and twenty four – or thereabouts", I bellowed the triumphant total from the top of the stepladder and looked round to see how the recipient of the good news was taking it. He was nowhere to be seen.

"Darling!" I bellowed. A head appeared, tortoise-like, from the ravine below the swimming pool wall. I repeated the news, and grabbed a branch of the tree to help myself down.

It sounds a fairly impressive total, and if we were picking peaches or pomegranates it would be. But you don't pick peaches in December and at that time our pomegranate tree was little more than a sapling. These were olives. So, not all that impressive then.

Productive olive trees are one of those quintessential Mediterranean staples. You inherit them, nurture them, re-plant them when necessary, harvest their bounty and admire their ancient beauty. As you sit with your bowl of garlicky olives, dipping your crusty bread in the oil, with a pitcher of local wine warming in the sun, you can reflect that Pericles may well have been doing the same as he discussed the finer details of the Parthenon with Phideas. And some of the trees you can see today may even have been alive then. It's an old crop.

Unfortunately we only have five trees, and they're not exactly patriarchs, they may just have been around to listen to Sartre, but hardly Socrates.

An olive farming friend once told me that if we really wanted olives for oil we'd need at least four kilos of fruit for every litre of oil. I scuttled into the kitchen to assess the Hauts Du Brel crop, and came to the dispiriting conclusion that we would hardly have enough to dress a small salad. Clearly they would have to be pickled.

Curing olives is an arcane process practised around the Mediterranean basin since earliest times. And since the easiest way to cure them is in a brine solution perhaps that's how it was discovered. The laden trees would drop their hard, bitter little fruits into the Aegean where they would float like a black raft on the warm, salty waters, and the constant, gentle pounding of the waves would automatically render them edible. I can't think how else it could have happened, because the taste of a raw uncured olive is quite execrable.

I decided to use the brining method for my own little harvest, and burrowed about in the cellars for a vast bag of coarse sea salt from Bayonne. Good salt and good pigs come from Bayonne. Add a sweet Quercynois melon and you have my favourite, simple and delicious summer *entrée* – but I digress.

I found a large mixing bowl, the sort my grandmother used to craft her exceptional cakes. Then I added a good handful of salt to a litre of cold water and rammed a plate down over the olives to keep the little blighters submerged. They popped out on all sides like chocolate covered popcorn. I ground my teeth and searched for a smaller container. A vast kilner jar caught my eye; it had recently been vacated by yesterday's lunch and was waiting to be filed away in a top cupboard by somebody a good foot taller than I am. An all purpose container, it proved to be the perfect receptacle for a small olive harvest. It took five and a half weeks of daily ministrations to effect the cure. Then I stored them in their jar, covered them with their own oil – or at least the oil from some of their Provençal cousins – and added a few peeled cloves of garlic, two whole chillies and a sprig of rosemary.

There is something innately satisfying about preserving olives from your own trees. You are practising an art that must have been perfected in these parts thousands of years ago, long before most other fruit and vegetables were available in Europe, and you can somehow feel the approval of the ancient Gods as you pour the wine and pass the bowl of lustrous, black bites.

They were absolutely glorious.

Since that first crop, my friend, Hélène has given me a proper olive jar, a beautiful terracotta pot with a yellow glaze. It's narrower at the top than the bottom – clever. So now my olives stand in their sunshine jar in a cool corner of the kitchen, always ready in case somebody pops in for an impromptu apero. Perhaps one day our trees will be large enough for us to collect a little oil, but I don't think I could ever give up the satisfaction of curing a few to offer with the wine and the cheese.

And I like to think Socrates would approve.

⋆

December is also the time for another typically Mediterranean crop, lemons. The lemon capital of France is a little town tucked away in the southeast corner of Provence, just this side of the Alps and a stone's throw from Italy. As it's situated right on the balmy Mediterranean it never gets frosted – or almost never – and has a phenomenally high rate of sunshine, perfect conditions for the golden citrus. The name Menton just exudes lemons. Nowadays though, they don't just export the fruit all over the world, they sell the trees too, little ones of course. It happens that Cahors is actually on about the same line of latitude as Menton – perhaps about 50kms north – the summers are just as balmy and hot and just as long; our problem is the freezing winters. But this never seemed to worry the great estates of France and Italy in their glory days; the trees were planted in huge terracotta pots and brought in to the *orangerie* or *limonaia* – a specially built greenhouse – for the winter. I decided to do the same. Our cellar, with its great glass double doors, would be a perfect substitute for their traditional wintering grounds, and in the summer they would grace the terrace. The thought of my own lemon trees was almost as heady as my own olives, and when faced with a cornucopia of jewel-encrusted saplings, my fertile compost heap of a mind went a little berserk. We now have four lemons, two limes, three clementines, a splendid kumquat and an orange. Well they weren't very big and I didn't know what my success rate would be. Naturally it was 100%. Of course if I'd only bought one tree the bally thing would have died within the week. I also didn't know how long it would take before I could expect any kind of crop, two lemons per tree maybe? That would be a good score for the first year, I thought, naively. By which you can see that I was woefully ignorant of my subject. The lemons produced about thirty fruits each, the limes and clementines about forty and the orange about twelve. As for the kumquats, they were innumerable. Hmmm, I thought, I might *possibly* have overdone it here...

We picked the clementines and oranges for Christmas, no problem there, not that year anyway. It'll be a bit more of a problem when the trees are eight feet tall, the cellar looks like a Rousseau painting and I have five hundred fruits to deal with. I haven't mentioned this disturbing little wrinkle in my fruit production plan to the beloved yet. He might make me sell them, or even give them away. I decided I'd better hone my marmalade-making skills before we arrive at that particular catalyst.

The limes were picked in very early December and wrapped in paper because they lose their glorious colour if you leave them – yet another thing I didn't know. The lemons were treated rather differently. Pick a few and leave a few on the tree, I was advised. As I generally use at least three lemons a week, even in winter, we decided to do just that. Thirty were picked and wrapped, ten came upstairs for culinary purposes and the rest were left on the trees to see what happened.

Meanwhile, I had eighty limes to deal with. There are only so many Thai dishes, Mexican salads and Mediterranean specialities one can reasonably be expected to consume in a year. I generally use a lime a week. Presuming they lasted the year – and even I knew they wouldn't – I had a surplus of at least thirty. Lime pickle was the answer. I made two batches, a classic Indian and an innovative, fruity Mediterranean.

The French are not terribly fond of pickled relishes, and sadly you just don't find them accompanying the vast terrines and *pâtés* they would set off so delectably. A cornichon is the southern Frenchman's exclusive nod towards pickles. Lime pickle however, turned out to be a perfect summer condiment; with a duck *pâté*, with slices of *jambon braisé* or with my very favourite, cold *poulet rôti*.

"Darling! You there? Is lunch ready yet?" Howled the beloved, from the lower terrace, where he was chopping wood.

I put a pot of the Mediterranean variety in the fridge to cool and set about assuaging his hunger pangs.

Lunch that day was a lingering affair, starting with a juicy sliced loin of pork *confit* – raked out from the spider-infested pool house that morning – and a vast tomato salad, drenched in lemon juice and olive oil. (We discovered that lime pickle accompanies pork splendidly) There was a ripe goat's cheese from the farms around Gramat on the high Causses, and the ubiquitous baguettes were warm from the baker's oven in Sauzet. There was a bowl of our own olives and a small jug of local wine from the small but pristine vineyards at Cenac – it was getting late and we weren't planning to work that afternoon anyway.

I felt yet another ridiculous glow of pride, almost amazement, that these olives came from our own trees and that I'd somehow managed to acquire the ancient know-how to render them edible. Picking up the warm country baguette I broke off a fair sized piece, rubbed the broken surface with a cut clove of garlic, dipped it in the greeny-gold salad oil, and took a delectable, lingering, mouth-watering bite.

This is the glorious Quercy, where olive oil, essence of the Mediterranean, meets the ambrosial food of southwestern France, perfectly complemented by the deliciously dark nectar that flows so freely in this region.

I'm not saying it's heaven, but it must run it pretty close.

★ ★ ★ ★ ★

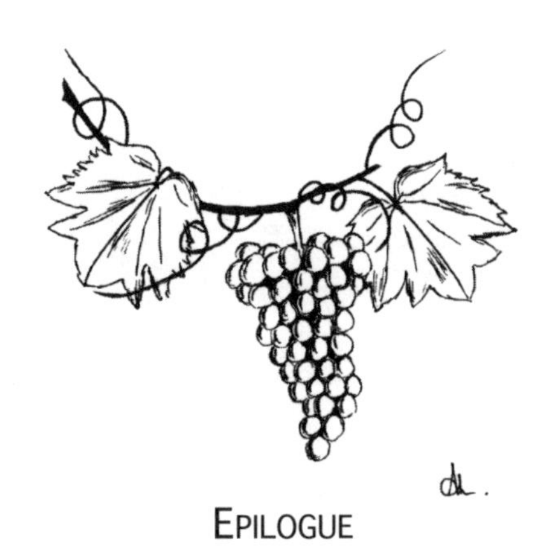

EPILOGUE

Late May and the upper terrace baked gently in the early afternoon sun. The beloved lay back in his chair and picked up his glass from a smooth hunk of rock doing temporary service as a drinks table. A small terracotta bowl of home-cured olives nudged a jug of dark local, the colour of elderberries.

"White stone, black wine," he grinned at me as he swirled the precious liquid, narrowly avoiding the unintentional baptism of his trousers.

The valley below was at lunch, still and silent but for the siren song of the cicadas, winding themselves up to high pitch.

The wonderful, evocative sound of warm southern Europe.

* * *